GRADE

3

Foundational Skills Workbook

Pearson Education, Inc., 330 Hudson Street, New York, NY 10013

Copyright © Pearson Education, Inc., or its affiliates. All rights Reserved. Printed in the United States of America. This publication is protected by copyright, and permission should be obtained from the publisher prior to any prohibited reproduction, storage in a retrieval system, or transmission in any form or by any means, electronic, mechanical, photocopying, recording, or likewise. For information regarding permissions, request forms, and the appropriate contacts within the Pearson Education Global Rights & Permissions department, please visit www.pearsoned.com/permissions.

PEARSON, ALWAYS LEARNING, and SCOTT FORESMAN are exclusive trademarks owned by Pearson Education, Inc., or its affiliates in the U.S. and/or other countries.

Unless otherwise indicated herein, any third-party trademarks that may appear in this work are the property of their respective owners and any references to third-party trademarks, logos or other trade dress are for demonstrative or descriptive purposes only. Such references are not intended to imply any sponsorship, endorsement, authorization, or promotion of Pearson's products by the owners of such marks, or any relationship between the owner and Pearson Education, Inc. or its affiliates, authors, licensees, or distributors.

PEARSON

PEARSON

ISBN-13: 978-0-328-96300-3
ISBN-10:   0-328-96300-3

3   18

Phonics

Spelling

Consonant Blends

Directions Read the story. Underline the words with the three-letter blends **squ, spl, thr,** and **str.** Then write the underlined words on the lines.

Emily threw on her coat
and ran down the street. As
she got to the town square,
she saw three friends throwing
water balloons at one another.
Each time a balloon struck the
ground, it split open. Water
splashed everywhere. Then
someone tossed a balloon
with such strength that it flew
through an open car window.
Emily knew they had to find
the owner and tell what they
had done.

1. _____
2. _____
3. _____
4. _____
5. _____
6. _____
7. _____
8. _____
9. _____
10. _____

Directions Read each word and listen for the three-letter blend. Then write two more words that start with the same blend. Underline the three-letter blend in each word you write.

11. straw _____ _____

12. splurge _____ _____

13. squeak _____ _____

14. thread _____ _____

15. straight _____ _____

© Pearson Education, Inc., 3

Home Activity Your child wrote words that begin with the three-letter blends *spl* (as in *splash*), *squ* (as in *square*), *str* (as in *strike*), and *thr* (as in *throw*). Challenge your child to name additional words that begin with these three-letter blends. For help in identifying words with these starting letters, you can use a di...

10

Name _____

Consonant Digraphs

Directions Write **sh, th, ph, ch, tch,** or **ng** to complete each word. Write the whole word on the line to the left.

_____ 1. Maria's family pur____ased a house.

_____ 2. Her mo____er decided to paint it.

_____ 3. She went to the store and bought bru____es and buckets.

_____ 4. When she came home she put on old clo____ing.

_____ 5. Then she pa____ed the cracks and nail holes.

_____ 6. Maria didn't know what color her room was goi____ to be.

_____ 7. She ____oned her friend to talk about it.

_____ 8. Her friend helped Maria make the ____oice.

_____ 9. Maria picked a beautiful ____ade of peach.

Directions Say the name of each picture. Write **sh, th, wh, ph, tch,** or **ng** to complete each word.

10. tro____y

11. wa____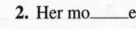

12. a____lete

13. ____ale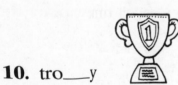

14. swi____

15. spla____

© Pearson Education, Inc., 3

Home Activity Your child wrote words with the consonants *sh* (English), *th* (father), *wh* (wheel), *ph* (trophy), *ch* (chapter), *tch* (watch), and *ng* (wing). Have your child read the words on the page above. Ask your child to change one or more letters in some of the words to form new words. For example, substituting *t* for *p* in *peach* forms *teach*.

School + Home

Contractions

Directions Use each pair of words to make a contraction. Write the contraction on the line.

_____ 1. have not

_____ 2. when is

_____ 3. did not

_____ 4. they will

_____ 5. she is

_____ 6. you will

_____ 7. we would

_____ 8. I would

_____ 9. let us

_____ 10. they are

_____ 11. that is

_____ 12. he would

_____ 13. was not

_____ 14. you would

Directions: Use the words in ( ) to make a contraction to complete each sentence. Write the contraction on the line.

_____ 15. Judy (has not) planted a garden before.

_____ 16. This year she decided (she would) like to grow some plants.

_____ 17. Her mom said that (they would) work together.

_____ 18. Judy's mom told her that it (was not) yet time to plant the garden.

_____ 19. She explained that seeds can't grow if (it is) too cold.

_____ 20. She also said that plants (would not) grow without water.

Home Activity Your child formed contractions by using an apostrophe to take the place of letters that are left out. Ask your child to think of at least ten other word pairs that can be used to form contractions, such as *she is (she's)*, *we will (we'll)*, and *are not (aren't)*. Ask your child to write sentences using these contractions.

Name _____

Prefixes *un-, re-, mis-, dis-, non-*

Directions Add the prefix **un-, re-, mis-, non-,** or **dis-** to each base word. Write the new word on the line.

1. un-   +   load   =   _____

2. re-   +   learn   =   _____

3. mis-   +   direct   =   _____

4. non-   +   sense   =   _____

5. dis-   +   like   =   _____

Directions Write the word from the box that best fits each definition.

_____ **6.** to spell wrong

_____ **7.** without stopping

_____ **8.** not known

_____ **9.** to write again

_____ **10.** not honest

> nonstop
> dishonest
> misspell
> rewrite
> unknown

Directions Add the prefix **un-, re-, mis-,** or **dis-** to the word in ( ) to complete each sentence. Write the new word on the line.

_____ **11.** Last night I was (able) to see the stars.

_____ **12.** The sky was so dark, I thought they had (appeared).

_____ **13.** I couldn't find the telescope. Someone had (placed) it.

_____ **14.** When I asked who had used the telescope last, no one could (call).

_____ **15.** It's (likely) that I will see the stars tonight.

© Pearson Education, Inc., 3

School + Home **Home Activity** Your child wrote words with the prefixes *un- (unhappy), re- (recall), mis- (mistake), non- (nonsense),* and *dis- (dislike).* Ask your child to choose words from the box above and use them in sentences. Then ask your child to remove the prefix from each word and use the new words in sentences.

Name _____

Spellings of /j/, /k/, /s/

Directions Underline the letter or letters that stand for the sound /j/ in **jar**, **large**, and **edge**. Then write a sentence using each word.

1. damage

_____

2. bridge

_____

3. banjo

_____

4. village

_____

Directions Circle the words in the box that have the sound /k/ spelled *k*, *c*, *ck*, and *ch* as in **mark**, **cost**, **pick**, and **school**. Write the words on the lines below.

> brake   branch   cellar   decide   locket
> merchant   peaceful   stomach   stretch   stuck

5. _____   **7.** _____

6. _____   **8.** _____

Directions Choose the words with the sound /s/ as in **person** and **pencil**. Write the word on the line.

_____   **9.** acid   is   picture

_____   **10.** become   catch   inside

_____   **11.** coat   dance   was

_____   **12.** account   bacon   once

Home Activity Your child wrote words with the /j/ sound in *jar*, *large*, and *edge*, the /s/ sound in *person* and *pencil*, and the /k/ sound in *mark*, *cost*, *pick*, and *chorus*. Encourage your child to identify other words with the /j/, /s/, or /k/ sounds. Together, make a list of these words and use them in sentences.

Name _____

Suffixes *-ly, -ful, -ness, -less, -able, -ible*

Directions Add the suffix **-ly, -ful, -ness, -able, -ible,** or **-less** to each base word. Write the new word on the line.

1. grace   +   -ful   =   _____

2. bare   +   -ly   =   _____

3. depend   +   -able   =   _____

4. fair   +   -ness   =   _____

5. convert   +   -ible   =   _____

6. wire   +   -less   =   _____

7. rare   +   -ly   =   _____

8. neat   +   -ness   =   _____

Directions Add **-ly, -ful, -ness, -able,** or **-less** to the base word in ( ) to best complete each sentence. Use the word box for help. Write the new word on the line.

> careful   careless   illness   quickly   safely   dependable   thickness

_____ 9. A (care) mistake can cause an oil spill at sea.

_____ 10. This can (quick) cause problems for seabirds.

_____ 11. We can all help, by being (depend).

_____ 12. If the oil is not (safe) removed, the birds cannot fly.

_____ 13. If a seabird swallows oil, it can develop an (ill).

_____ 14. The (thick) of a bird's eggshell can also change.

_____ 15. To protect the sea and its wildlife, ships' captains must be (care).

© Pearson Education, Inc., 3

Home Activity Your child wrote words with the suffixes *-ly (safely)*, *-ful (playful)*, *-ness (illness)*, and *-less (worthless)*. Name some base words such as *slow, thank, harm, kind,* and *help*. Ask your child to make new words using the suffixes he or she practiced on this page.

Consonant Patterns *wr, kn, gn, st, mb*

Directions Choose the word in ( ) with the silent consonant, as in **wr, kn, st, mb,** or **gn,** to complete each sentence. Write the word on the line.

_____ **1.** It seemed like the perfect winter day for a (climb/hike) up the mountain.

_____ **2.** Jan packed water and snacks in a (cooler/knapsack).

_____ **3.** She put on her coat and (knit/new) cap.

_____ **4.** She grabbed the scarf with the blue and yellow (design/stripes).

_____ **5.** Then she (tossed/wrapped) it around her neck.

_____ **6.** Jan began to (close/fasten) her coat.

_____ **7.** The radio was on, and Jan stopped to (hear/listen).

_____ **8.** The reporter said there were (calls/signs) that a big snowstorm was on its way.

_____ **9.** Jan (learned/knew) she would have to go hiking another day.

Directions Circle each word in the box that has a silent consonant. Write the circled words in alphabetical order on the lines below.

gnaw relax castle wrong basket no comb knot humid water trap numb

10. _____   **13.** _____

11. _____   **14.** _____

12. _____   **15.** _____

Home Activity Your child wrote words with the silent consonants *wr (write), kn (knight), st (listen), mb (thumb),* and *gn (gnaw).* Work with your child to see how many words with those silent letters you can name together. Write the words and take turns making sentences using each word.

Irregular Plurals

Directions Use the plural form of each word in ( ) to complete each sentence.
Write the word on the line.

_____ 1. Timmy wasn't like the other (mouse).

_____ 2. He was missing all his (tooth).

_____ 3. He couldn't chew into the (loaf) of bread in the bakery
where he lived.

_____ 4. Using his (foot) to pull off tiny pieces of bread didn't
work.

_____ 5. Of course the (woman) who worked in the bakery would
never feed him.

_____ 6. When the delivery (man) came, Timmy would run and
hide.

_____ 7. Timmy finally solved his problem when he saw some
(child) dropping crumbs.

_____ 8. Now he stores the crumbs behind the (shelf) so he can eat
them whenever he wants.

Directions Write the plural form of each word below.

9. wife _____   15. banjo _____

10. wolf _____   16. elf _____

11. scarf _____   17. half _____

12. hero _____   18. goose _____

13. cuff _____   19. knife _____

14. calf _____   20. sheep _____

School + Home

Home Activity Your child wrote plurals—words naming more than one person, place, or thing. Ask your
child to review the plural forms of the words on the page above. Work together to write a silly poem or song
using these and other plural words.

Vowels: *r*-Controlled /ėr/

Directions Circle the words in the box that have the vowel sound /ėr/ as in **bird, her, turn, earn,** and **work.** Then write the words you circled under the word that has the same vowel spelling.

burst	**hear**	**corn**	**dear**	**early**	**there**	**fern**
fire	**flare**	**heart**	**girl**	**hurry**	**learn**	**pear**
perch	**skirt**	**tire**	**torn**	**world**	**worm**	

bird

1. _____

2. _____

her

3. _____

4. _____

turn

5. _____

6. _____

earn

7. _____

8. _____

work

9. _____

10. _____

Directions Circle the word that has the same vowel sound as the first word. Then write a sentence that uses the word you circled.

11. **farm**   frame   dart   rare

_____

12. **short**   hoot   horn   shot

_____

13. **core**   cone   to   shore

_____

14. **board**   boat   proud   roar

_____

Home Activity Your child identified and wrote words with *r*-controlled vowels. With your child, write sentences for the answer words from items 1-10 above. Ask your child to underline the letters that stand for /ėr/.

Name _____

Prefixes *pre-, mid-, over-, bi-, out-, de-*

Directions Add the prefix **pre-, mid-, over-, out-,** or **de-** to each base word. Write the new word on the line.

1. over- + load = _____

2. out- + going = _____

3. pre- + paid = _____

4. mid- + point = _____

5. de- + code = _____

Directions Choose the word from the box that best fits the definition. Write the word on the line.

_____ **6.** a word part added to the beginning of a word

_____ **7.** a vehicle with two wheels

_____ **8.** bursting forth

_____ **9.** the middle of the week

_____ **10.** to thaw something that is frozen

> **bicycle**
> **midweek**
> **outburst**
> **defrost**
> **prefix**

Directions Add the prefix **pre-, mid-, over-, bi-,** or **out-** to the base word in ( ) to complete each sentence. Write the word on the line.

_____ **11.** Elena began to collect rocks when she was in (school).

_____ **12.** She thought this hobby would (last) any of her other hobbies.

_____ **13.** It is easy to (look) rocks during the day.

_____ **14.** She found a (color) rock one day.

_____ **15.** Finding them at (night) is nearly impossible.

Home Activity Your child formed and wrote words with the prefixes *pre-, mid-, over-, bi-, out-,* and *de-.* Work together to list other words with these prefixes, such as *pretest, midway, overhead, bilingual, outgrow,* and *deflate.* Have your child use each word in a sentence.

© Pearson Education, Inc., 3

Name _____

Suffixes -*er*, -*or*, -*ess*, -*ist*

Directions Add the suffix to each base word. Write the new word on the line.

1. edit   +   -or   =   _____

2. art   +   -ist   =   _____

3. conduct   +   -or   =   _____

4. lion   +   -ess   =   _____

5. sell   +   -er   =   _____

Directions Write the word from the box that best fits each definition.

_____ **6.** a doctor who cares for your teeth

_____ **7.** one who ships packages

_____ **8.** one who directs

_____ **9.** a scientist in the field of chemistry

_____ **10.** a woman who greets restaurant guests

> **chemist**
> **dentist**
> **hostess**
> **shipper**
> **director**

Directions Add the suffix **-er**, **-or**, **-ess**, or **-ist** to the base word in ( ) to complete each sentence. Use the words in the box to help. Write the word on the line.

_____ **11.** Gertrude Ederle was the first woman (swim) to swim across the English Channel.

_____ **12.** Many thought her coach was the greatest swimming (instruct) in the world.

_____ **13.** After she became famous, Ederle was offered work as an (act), but she declined.

_____ **14.** Instead, she traveled as a (tour).

_____ **15.** Later, Ederle became a swimming (teach) for deaf children.

> **actress**
> **instructor**
> **swimmer**
> **teacher**
> **tourist**

Home Activity Your child formed and wrote words with the suffixes -*er*, -*or*, -*ess*, and -*ist*. Together, think of additional job-related words that end with -*er*, -*or*, -*ess*, or -*ist* (such as *doctor, countess, biologist, police officer*). Help your child write a paragraph explaining which jobs sound most interesting to him or her and why.

Name _____

Syllables VCCCV

Directions Choose the word in ( ) with the VCCCV syllable pattern to finish each sentence. Write the word on the line.

_____ 1. The third grade (children/students) took a trip to the zoo.

_____ 2. Their teachers had a (surprise/special) assignment for them.

_____ 3. The zookeeper gave an (alert/address) to the students.

_____ 4. He told them to (inspect/watch) each animal's living space.

_____ 5. He suggested they (compare/contrast) different animals.

_____ 6. By the end of the day, the students had seen about one (dozen/hundred) animals.

Directions Circle the word that has the VCCCV syllable pattern. Then write a sentence on the line that uses the word you circled.

7. forgive   monster   wonder

_____

8. human   fortress   winner

_____

9. complain   number   writer

_____

10. constant   planet   signal

_____

11. beyond   robin   sample

_____

12. chosen   control   copper

_____

Home Activity Your child wrote words with the VCCCV syllable pattern found in *mon/ster*. Ask your child to read each of the words he or she wrote on the page above. Take turns making up additional sentences using these words. Help your child write the sentences and underline the words with the VCCCV syllable pattern.

Syllable Pattern CV/VC

Directions Circle the word with two vowels together where each vowel has a separate vowel sound. Then underline the letters that stand for the two different vowel sounds.

1. clean   paint   patio

2. audio   faith   search

3. greed   journal   rodeo

4. either   medium   southern

5. beach   pound   pioneer

6. duo   poison   waiter

7. grain   group   stadium

8. mean   freeze   video

Directions Read the paragraph. Circle all the underlined words with two vowels together where each vowel has a separate vowel sound. Write the words on the lines below.

> Marie was <u>eager</u> to <u>create</u> a new song. She <u>thought</u> she had an <u>idea</u> for a tune. She <u>tried</u> it on the <u>piano</u>. Then she wrote a part for the <u>violin</u>. She liked the way it <u>sounded</u>. Marie invited three <u>friends</u> to go to the <u>studio</u> with her. Her <u>friends</u> were singers. Marie <u>explained</u> the music. The <u>trio</u> made a <u>stereo</u> recording. Someday you might even hear it on the <u>radio</u>.

9. _____   10. _____

11. _____   12. _____

13. _____   14. _____

15. _____   16. _____

Home Activity Your child identified and wrote words in which two vowels together each stand for a separate vowel sound, as in *stereo* and *stadium*. Ask your child to read the words aloud from the page above. Have your child name the long vowel sounds in each word.

Homophones

Directions Choose the word that best matches each definition. Write the word on the line.

_____ **1.** a small room in a prison   sell   cell

_____ **2.** to record on paper   right   write

_____ **3.** 60 minutes   hour   our

_____ **4.** not strong   weak   week

_____ **5.** a period of darkness   knight   night

_____ **6.** swallowed   ate   eight

_____ **7.** a story   tail   tale

_____ **8.** also   to   too

Directions Choose the best word to complete each sentence. Write the word on the line.

_____ **9.** My aunt (cent/sent) us a letter.

_____ **10.** I did not (hear/here) you.

_____ **11.** The letter said my aunt would (meat/meet) us at the airport.

_____ **12.** Our (plain/plane) arrived late.

_____ **13.** We looked everywhere and did not (sea/see) my aunt.

_____ **14.** Finally (eye/I) spotted her near the baggage claim area.

_____ **15.** Then we (knew/new) everything would be fine in our new country.

© Pearson Education, Inc., 3

Home Activity Your child identified and wrote homophones—words that sound the same but have different meanings and spellings. Work with your child to make a list of other homophones, such as *for/four, heard/herd, sail/sale,* and *one/won.* Take turns writing sentences that correctly use each homophone.

Vowel Patterns *a, au, aw, al, augh, ough*

Directions Choose the word with the vowel sound in **ball**. Write the word on the line.

_____ 1. We moved (because/when) we wanted to live near family.

_____ 2. Now we live in a (little/small) apartment.

_____ 3. Mom works hard so that someday we can buy a house with a (lawn/yard).

_____ 4. Sometimes we (speak/talk) about our old home.

_____ 5. We think about the beautiful land and the (banana/palm) trees that grew everywhere.

_____ 6. We (caught/found) fish in the ocean every day.

_____ 7. We miss some things, but we (always/still) agree that we are glad we came to this country.

_____ 8. In this country, we found what we (needed/sought).

Directions Write **a, au, aw, al, augh** or **ough** to complete each word. Use the word box to help you. Write the whole word on the line before the sentence.

| cough | automobile | sausage | shawl | taught | walk | walnut |

_____ 9. I picture my grandmother in her rocker, wearing a purple sh_____l around her shoulders.

_____ 10. I remember the scent of warm w_____lnut rolls.

_____ 11. I miss the s_____sage she cooked for our dinner.

_____ 12. It was so good and spicy that it made me c_____.

_____ 13. But it was my grandmother who t_____t us to enjoy what we have now.

_____ 14. We can w_____k around freely wherever we want.

_____ 15. We even have our own _____tomobile.

Home Activity Your child identified and wrote words with the vowel sound in *ball* as in *small, because, lawn, talk, taught,* and *cough.* Work together to write a list of words that rhyme with these words. Then have your child write sentences that include words on the list.

Name _____

Vowel Patterns *ei, eigh*

Directions Read each sentence. Underline the word that has *ei* or *eigh*. Write *long a,* *long e,* or *long i* on the line to tell what sound the vowel pattern stands for.

_____ 1. We enjoy shopping at our neighborhood bakery.

_____ 2. We always go on either Friday or Saturday.

_____ 3. Shelves of baked goods reach from floor to ceiling.

_____ 4. I'm not the right height yet to reach the top shelf.

_____ 5. That shelf must be eight feet high!

_____ 6. We weigh all our choices and make up our minds.

_____ 7. We smile when we receive our package from the salesclerk.

Directions Choose a word from the box to match each clue. Write the word on the line.

_____ 8. a strap used to control a horse

_____ 9. to grab an object

_____ 10. free time

_____ 11. a person who lives nearby

_____ 12. the space between something's lowest and highest point

_____ 13. cargo carried from one place to another by truck, ship, or other vehicle

_____ 14. not tell the truth

_____ 15. a blood vessel in a living creature's body

| deceive |
| freight |
| height |
| leisure |
| neighbor |
| rein |
| seize |
| vein |

© Pearson Education, Inc., 3

School + Home

Home Activity Your child identified and used words with the long *a, e,* or *i* sound spelled *ei* or *eigh*. Work together to make a crossword puzzle, beginning with words and definitions from this page.

Suffixes -y, -ish, -hood, -ment

Directions Combine the base word and suffix. Write the new word on the line.

1. pay   +   -ment   =   _____

2. cloud   +   -y   =   _____

3. self   +   -ish   =   _____

4. boy   +   -hood   =   _____

5. storm   +   -y   =   _____

6. excite   +   -ment   =   _____

7. false   +   -hood   =   _____

8. baby   +   -ish   =   _____

Directions Add **-y, -ish, -hood,** or **-ment** to the base word in ( ) to best complete each sentence. Use the word box for help. Write the new word on the line.

> **childhood**   **entertainment**   **foolish**   **frosty**
> **movement**   **neighborhood**   **snowy**

_____ 9. During my (child) we moved often.

_____ 10. We moved to a (neighbor) with woods and a pond nearby.

_____ 11. Playing outdoors provided plenty of (entertain).

_____ 12. One (snow) day, my brother and I decided to go skating.

_____ 13. We were scared by (move) along the edge of the pond.

_____ 14. How (fool) we felt when we saw it was Ben, our new neighbor.

_____ 15. We thought it was a (frost) snowman come to life.

School + Home **Home Activity** Your child added the suffixes -y, -ish, -hood, and -ment to base words to form new words. Work together to form other words with these suffixes, such as *thirsty, childish,* and *shipment.* Have your child write sentences using the new words.

Name _____

Vowel Sounds in *moon* and *foot*

Directions Circle each word with the vowel sound in **moon** or the vowel sound in **foot**. Then write each word in the correct column.

1. Our school took us on a field trip to an art museum.

2. We spent a full day studying famous paintings and statues.

3. We looked at works by some of the art world's true masters.

4. After we returned to class, our teacher asked us to make a new drawing in our notebooks.

5. I sketched a picture of President Lincoln wearing a black wool suit and a very tall hat.

vowel sound in moon

6. _____

7. _____

8. _____

9. _____

10. _____

vowel sound in foot

11. _____

12. _____

13. _____

14. _____

15. _____

Directions Cross out the one word in each line that does **not** have the vowel sound in **moon** or the vowel sound in **foot**.

16. build   cushion   glue

17. bushel   rocket   smooth

18. button   bookstore   juice

19. football   stew   story

20. balloon   pudding   throat

Home Activity Your child identified and wrote words with the vowel sounds in *moon* (as in *school, new, glue,* and *fruit*) and *foot* (as in *cookie* and *cushion*). Have your child write riddles using words with the vowel sounds in *moon* and *foot*. Try to guess the answer after your child reads each riddle to you.

Schwa spelled with an *a, e, i, o, u,* and *y*

Directions Choose the word with a vowel that has the same sound as the underlined vowels in **a̲bout**, **tak̲en**, **penc̲il**, **lem̲on**, **circ̲us**, and **Sib̲yl** to complete each sentence. Write the word on the line to the left.

_____ **1.** Susan was (afraid/scared) to walk her dog without a leash.

_____ **2.** Every time she opened the front door, the little (pooch/rascal) ran off.

_____ **3.** One time she took her dog to a (local/nearby) park.

_____ **4.** All the (animals/doggies) were fetching or chasing.

_____ **5.** Susan removed her puppy's (vinyl/nylon) leash and let the dog run freely.

_____ **6.** When her dog ran off, Susan opened a (paper/plastic) bag and pulled out a treat.

_____ **7.** Susan's dog quickly (traveled/bounded) back.

_____ **8.** Now anytime Susan offers her dog a tasty (biscuit/morsel), it comes racing to her.

Directions Circle the letter in each word that stands for the same sound as the underlined vowels in **a̲bout**, **tak̲en**, **penc̲il**, **lem̲on**, **circ̲us**, and **Sib̲yl**.

9. kitchen	**12.** family	**15.** vinyl	**18.** ago
10. river	**13.** melon	**16.** dollar	**19.** open
11. surprise	**14.** sugar	**17.** nickel	**20.** canyon

Home Activity Your child identified and wrote words that contain the vowel sound called schwa, heard in words with unaccented syllables such as *about, taken, pencil, lemon, circus,* and *Sibyl*. Help your child write sentences with words that have this sound. Ask your child to read each sentence and identify the letter that stands for the schwa sound.

Final Syllables *-tion, -ion, -ture, -ive, -ize*

Directions Circle the correctly spelled word in each pair.

1. commosion   commotion
2. invasion   invation
3. generasion   generation
4. posision   position
5. relaxasion   relaxation
6. division   divition
7. vacasion   vacation
8. explotion   explosion

Directions Add **-ture, -ive,** or **-ize** to complete each word below. Write the complete word on the line. (HINT: there is only one correct choice for each word.)

9. pas _____
10. act _____
11. rup _____
12. mass _____
13. maxim _____
14. real _____
15. cap _____
16. adven _____

Directions Choose four words from the above list and write a sentence for each word.

17. _____
18. _____
19. _____
20. _____

© Pearson Education, Inc., 3

Home Activity Your child identified and wrote words that end with the syllables *-tion, -ion, -ture, -ive,* and *-ize.* Work together to write sentences using the words from the page above. Ask your child to underline the final syllable in the words used from this page.

Prefixes *im-, in-*

Directions For each definition, write a word on the line that beings with **im-** or **in-**.

1. not mature _____

2. not efficient _____

3. not sincere _____

4. not polite _____

5. not perfect _____

6. not mortal _____

7. not adequate _____

8. not capable _____

9. not partial _____

10. not possible _____

11. not correct _____

12. not direct _____

13. not practical _____

14. not probable _____

15. not pure _____

Directions Now write three sentences of your own. In each sentence include at least one of the **im-** or **in-** words from above.

16. _____

17. _____

18. _____

© Pearson Education, Inc., 3

Home Activity Your child used words with the prefixes *im-* and *in-*, which mean "not." Read a newspaper or magazine article with your child. Point out words with the prefixes *im-* and *in-* and have your child explain what they mean.

School + Home

Related Words

Directions Choose the word that best matches each clue. Write the word on the line.

1. coverings for the body   (cloth   clothes)   _____

2. a person who plays sports   (athlete   athletics)   _____

3. a person's handwritten name   (sign   signature)   _____

4. a tub for washing   (bath   bathe)   _____

5. the world of living things and the outdoors   (natural   nature)   _____

Directions Read each pair of related words. Underline the parts that are spelled the same but pronounced differently. Write a sentence using one of the words in each pair.

6. feel   felt _____

7. keep   kept _____

8. decide   decision _____

9. mean   meant _____

10. define   definition _____

11. volcano   volcanic _____

12. please   pleasant _____

13. relate   relative _____

14. sign   signal _____

15. repeat   repetition _____

School + Home

Home Activity Your child read and wrote related words that have parts that are spelled the same but pronounced differently, as in *cloth* and *clothes*. Discuss the meanings of the related words on the page above. Then work together to write a story that uses some of the words.

© Pearson Education, Inc., 3

Name _____

Vowel Digraphs

Rhymes Write the list word that rhymes with the underlined word.

Spelling Words

clean
agree
teeth
dream
grain
coach
display
window

shadow
cheese
peach
braid
Sunday
float
thrown

1. Did you ever meet a <u>goat</u> that knew how to _____ ?

2. Did you ever <u>approach</u> the other team's _____ ?

3. Did you ever <u>reach</u> for a big fuzzy _____ ?

4. Did you ever get a <u>pain</u> from eating green _____ ?

5. Did you ever <u>scream</u> when you had a bad _____ ?

6. Did you ever help <u>Jean</u> keep her room _____ ?

7. Did you ever get <u>paid</u> to wear your hair in a _____ ?

Context Clues Write the missing list word.

8. I like grilled _____ sandwiches.

9. Floss your _____ every day.

10. The first day of the week is _____ .

11. The tree cast a long _____ .

12. Let's open the _____ to get some fresh air.

13. Mom will _____ to drive us to the game.

14. I've _____ out all my old papers.

15. Let's make a _____ of our seashells.

Home Activity Your child wrote words with long vowel digraphs (letter combinations that stand for long vowel sounds). Ask your child to circle the digraphs *ai*, *ay*, *ee*, *ea*, *oa*, and *ow*.

© Pearson Education, Inc., 3

37

Vowel Digraphs

Proofread a Description Circle five misspelled words in Amy's description. Circle the word with a capitalization error. Write the words correctly.

> I can see a troll from my window. He has realy big teath and a long braid down his back. At night, I watch him dreem under the tree or flote in the moonlight. mom says he's just a shado, but I don't always agree.

1. _____   2. _____

3. _____   4. _____

5. _____   6. _____

Proofread Words Fill in the circle to show the correctly spelled word.

7. The model train was on _____ .
   ○ displaiy   ○ display   ○ dissplay   ○ displaye

8. We are going to the lake on _____ .
   ○ sunday   ○ Sundaye   ○ Sundai   ○ Sunday

9. Our _____ bought treats after the game.
   ○ coach   ○ coche   ○ coash   ○ cowch

10. Everyone helped _____ the garage.
   ○ kleen   ○ cleen   ○ clean   ○ klean

© Pearson Education, Inc., 3

School + Home   **Home Activity** Your child spelled words with long vowel digraphs (letter combinations that make long vowel sounds). Take turns with your child spelling a list word and using it in a sentence.

38

14/
/14

Compound Words

Proofread a Description Ann wrote about a family
reunion. Underline two words that should have been
a compound word. Circle three other spelling mistakes.
Write the words correctly. Add the missing comma.

All my relatives met at a camp ground.
The grownups talked while the kids
played football and chased butterflys.
Then evryone ate chicken, popcorn,
bluebery pie, and other good food.
Nobody wanted to say goodnight.

1. _camground_   2. _everyone_
3. _butterflies_ 4. _blueberry_

Proofread Words Fill in the circle to show the
correctly spelled word.

5. Our family always has ____ on Sunday night.
   ● popcorn   ○ pop korn   ○ pop corn

6. Manuel's grandma has a ____ in her garden.
   ● scarecrow   ○ scarcrow   ○ scare crow

7. I do my ____ right after school.
   ○ homwork   ○ home work   ● homework

8. Let's build a castle in the ____ .
   ● sandbox   ○ sand box   ○ sandbocks

Spelling Words

sunglasses
football
homework
haircut
popcorn
railroad
snowstorm
earring

scarecrow
blueberry
butterflies
lawnmower
campground
sandbox
toothbrush

Frequently Misspelled Words

outside
everyone
something
sometimes

School + Home **Home Activity** Your child identified misspelled compound words. Have your child draw a line to divide each list word into its two parts.

49

Name _____

Words with *spl, thr, squ, str, scr*

Spelling Words				
splash	throw	three	square	scream
strike	street	split	splurge	thrill
strength	squeak	throne	scratch	squeeze

Rhyming Pairs Finish the sentence with a list word that rhymes with the underlined word.

1. He has a <u>batch</u> of itches to _____ .

2. Skiing down that <u>hill</u> was a _____ !

3. I don't think he has the _____ to swim the <u>length</u> of the pool.

4. See if you can _____ the ball to the <u>row</u> of trees.

5. The town _____ was <u>bare</u>.

6. The _____ has been occupied by six men and a <u>lone</u> woman.

7. There are _____ squirrels playing in the <u>tree</u>.

8. Let's <u>dash</u> into the water and make a big _____ .

Missing Blends Add a three-letter blend to finish the list word. Write the word.

9. The scared girl let out a ___ ___ ___ eam.   9. _____

10. The pitcher threw a ___ ___ ___ ike.   10. _____

11. Don't play in the ___ ___ ___ eet.   11. _____

12. I'd love to ___ ___ ___ urge on an expensive gift.   12. _____

13. Let's ___ ___ ___ it the last piece of pizza.   13. _____

14. Mom gave my hand a big ___ ___ ___ eeze.   14. _____

15. We heard the hinges ___ ___ ___ eak.   15. _____

School + Home

Home Activity Your child wrote words with three-letter blends (*spl, thr, squ, str,* and *scr*). Have your child circle and pronounce the three-letter blends in the list words.

Name _____

Words with *spl, thr, squ, str, scr*

Proofread a Report Circle four spelling mistakes in this report about the gray fox. Write the words correctly. Write the word that should be used instead of **don't** in the last sentence.

> A gray fox has a white belly. It can run fast and climb trees. It may splash into the water and swim if it is skared and needs to escape. It can also let out a high-pitched screem. When hunting, it listens for the sqeak of a mouse. If it sees movement, it srikes quickly. Sometimes, in bad weather, a gray fox don't leave its den for three or four days.

1. _____   2. _____

3. _____   4. _____

5. _____

Proofread Words Fill in the circle to show the correctly spelled word.

6. O thril   O thrill   O thill

7. O squeze   O sqeeze   O squeeze

8. O scatch   O scratch   O scrach

9. O throne   O trone   O throan

10. O stength   O strentgh   O strength

11. O streat   O steet   O street

12. O sqare   O square   O squar

© Pearson Education, Inc., 3

School + Home **Home Activity** Your child identified misspelled words with three-letter blends (*spl, thr, squ, str* and *scr*). Ask your child to use some of the list words to tell a story about a mouse.

Consonant Digraphs

Spelling Words				
father	chapter	other	alphabet	watch
English	weather	catch	fashion	shrink
pitcher	flash	athlete	trophy	nephew

Rhyme Clues Read the clue. Write the list word.

1. It rhymes with *patch,* but starts like *can.* _____

2. It rhymes with *link,* but starts like *shred.* _____

3. It rhymes with *feather,* but starts like *win.* _____

4. It rhymes with *mother,* but starts like *olive.* _____

5. It rhymes with *dash,* but starts like *flag.* _____

6. It rhymes with *stitcher,* but starts like *pencil.* _____

Making Connections Write a list word to fit each definition.

7. It's a list of letters. _____

8. It's something you might win. _____

9. It's a parent. It's not a mother. _____

10. It helps you tell the time. _____

11. It's a section of a book. _____

12. It's a sister's child. It's not a girl. _____

13. It's often spoken in Australia. _____

14. It could be a swimmer, a boxer, or a gymnast. _____

15. It's a trend in clothing. _____

© Pearson Education, Inc., 3

School + Home **Home Activity** Your child wrote words with *sh, th, ph, ch,* and *tch.* Point to a list word on this page. Ask your child to read the word and then look away and spell it correctly.

Name _____

Consonant Digraphs

Proofread Safety Tips Chad wrote some weather safety tips. Circle four spelling mistakes and one capitalization error. Write the words correctly.

➜ Don't let bad weatter cach you off guard. Listen to the forecast.

➜ Be ready to go to a basement if their is a tornado watch.

➜ Take shelter when you hear thunder. Don't wait for a flash of lightning.

➜ wear a cap, mittens, and othr warm clothes in freezing weather.

Spelling Words

father
chapter
other
alphabet
watch
English
weather
catch

fashion
shrink
pitcher
flash
athlete
trophy
nephew

1. _____   2. _____
3. _____   4. _____
5. _____

Proofread Words Circle the correctly spelled word. Write the word.

Frequently Misspelled Words

they
there
their

6. fashsun	fashion	6. _____
7. pitcher	picher	7. _____
8. trophy	trofy	8. _____
9. english	English	9. _____
10. shrink	shink	10. _____
11. atlete	athlete	11. _____
12. alpabet	alphabet	12. _____

Home Activity Your child identified misspelled words with *sh, th, ph, ch,* and *tch*. Have your child underline and pronounce these letter combinations in the list words.

Name _____

Syllables V/CV, VC/V

Spelling Words				
finish	pilot	even	wagon	music
silent	rapid	female	lemon	pupil
focus	robot	tulip	camel	salad

Crossword Puzzle Read each clue. Write the list word in the puzzle.

Across
2. to complete something
4. an animal with one or more humps
5. a sour fruit
8. a person who flies a plane
10. often made with lettuce
12. a kind of machine
13. very fast

Down
1. not odd but ___
2. the opposite of *male*
3. make no noise
6. songs
7. a toy with four wheels
8. a student
9. a spring flower
11. to adjust a camera lens

© Pearson Education, Inc., 3

Home Activity Your child has been learning to spell words with long and short vowel sounds with these syllable patterns: V/CV VC/V. Give clues about a word from the list. Ask your child to guess the word and then spell it.

Final Syllable -*le*

Rhymes Write the list word that rhymes with the word shown.

1. nickel   __ __ __ __ __ __

2. doodle   __ __ __ __ __ __

3. label   __ __ __ __ __

4. paddle   __ __ __ __ __ __

5. bubble   __ __ __ __ __ __

6. steeple   __ __ __ __ __ __

7. fiddle   __ __ __ __ __ __

8. dimple   __ __ __ __ __ __

Missing Words Write the list word that completes each phrase.

9. a door _____

10. not rough but _____

11. a barking _____

12. not my aunt but my _____

13. sit in the _____

14. _____ the balls

15. just a _____ bit more

handle	poodle
little	uncle
gentle	middle
juggle	

School + Home   **Home Activity** Your child is learning to spell words that end in -*le*. Together, say each word, spell it, clap, and loudly say "l, e" when you get to the end of a word.

Name _____

Compound Words

sunglasses	football	homework	haircut	popcorn
railroad	snowstorm	earring	scarecrow	blueberry
butterflies	lawnmower	campground	sandbox	toothbrush

Compound Match Up Draw a line to connect two words to make a compound word. Write the compound word.

1. tooth	corn	**1.** _____
2. pop	mower	**2.** _____
3. ear	berry	**3.** _____
4. lawn	brush	**4.** _____
5. foot	ring	**5.** _____
6. blue	work	**6.** _____
7. home	cut	**7.** _____
8. sand	ball	**8.** _____
9. rail	road	**9.** _____
10. hair	box	**10.** _____

Dividing Compounds Draw a line between the two words in each compound word. Write each word.

11. snowstorm   **11.** _____ + _____

12. campground   **12.** _____ + _____

13. sunglasses   **13.** _____ + _____

14. scarecrow   **14.** _____ + _____

15. butterflies   **15.** _____ + _____

© Pearson Education, Inc., 3

Home Activity Your child has been spelling compound words. Together, look for compound words in a favorite book. Ask your child to name the two words that make up each compound word.

Name _____

Words with *spl, thr, squ, str, scr*

Spelling Words				
splash	throw	three	square	scream
strike	street	split	splurge	thrill
strength	squeak	throne	scratch	squeeze

Question Clues Write the list word that answers each question.

1. How do you stop an itch?   1. _____

2. What is the name of that shape?   2. _____

3. What sound does a mouse make?   3. _____

4. Where does a queen sit?   4. _____

5. Where might you park a car?   5. _____

6. What might you do at a haunted house?   6. _____

7. What does a pitcher do with a ball?   7. _____

8. What number comes before four?   8. _____

9. What is it called when a batter swings
   and misses?   9. _____

10. What do you do to get toothpaste out of
    a tube?   10. _____

Proofreading Circle the list word that is spelled correctly. Write it.

11. splesh   splash   11. _____

12. thrill   thril   12. _____

13. stregth   strength   13. _____

14. splutt   split   14. _____

15. splurge   splurje   15. _____

Home Activity Your child learned words with the three-letter blends *spl, thr, squ, str,* and *scr.*
Divide a sheet of paper into four sections. Ask your child to sort and write the words according to
their beginning blends.

Name _____

Consonant Digraphs

Meaning Clues Read the clue. Write the list word the clue tells about. The letters in the boxes will answer this riddle:

What do you call cheese that's not yours?

1. get smaller   ___ ___ ___ ___ □ ___

2. the ABCs   ___ ___ □ ___ ___ ___ ___ ___

3. a clock for the wrist   ___ ___ □ ___ ___

4. a prize   ___ ___ □ ___ ___ ___

5. a clothing trend   ___ ___ □ ___ ___ ___ ___

6. something that can hold water   ___ ___ □ ___ ___ ___ ___

7. not a niece but a _____   ___ ___ ___ □ ___ ___ ___

8. a dad   ___ ___ □ ___ ___ ___

9. part of a book   ___ ___ □ ___ ___ ___ ___

10. a language   ___ ___ □ ___ ___ ___ ___

11. what it's like outside   ___ ___ □ ___ ___ ___ ___

Word Parts Write the list word that contains each small word.

12. ash   ___ ___ ___ ___ ___

13. her   ___ ___ ___ ___ ___

14. let   ___ ___ ___ ___ ___ ___ ___

15. cat   ___ ___ ___ ___ ___

© Pearson Education, Inc., 3

Contractions

Spelling Words				
let's	he'd	you'll	can't	I'd
won't	haven't	hasn't	she'd	they'll
when's	we'd	should've	wasn't	didn't

Contractions Write the underlined words as a contraction.

1. I wish <u>she had</u> stayed a few more days.

1. _____

2. If <u>you will</u> build a doghouse, I'll paint it.

2. _____

3. I <u>will not</u> be going to the party.

3. _____

4. I <u>can not</u> reach the top shelf.

4. _____

5. He <u>did not</u> go to the library.

5. _____

6. I knew <u>we had</u> put too much water in the paint.

6. _____

7. She <u>has not</u> finished writing the invitations.

7. _____

8. We <u>have not</u> played softball since Monday.

8. _____

Joining Words Write the contraction.

9. let + us

9. _____

10. they + will

10. _____

11. he + would

11. _____

12. when + is

12. _____

13. should + have

13. _____

14. was + not

14. _____

15. I + would

15. _____

© Pearson Education, Inc., 3

Home Activity Your child wrote contractions. Pronounce a list word. Have your child name the words that were combined and then spell the contraction.

Name _____

Contractions

Proofread a Report To find out what happened in a playground accident, Tim's teacher had everyone write about it. Circle four spelling mistakes in Tim's report. Write the words correctly. Rewrite the compound sentence with a comma.

I havn't been playing ball lately, so I did'nt see the accident with the bat. I was playing tag with Dan. He said hed been playing ball earlier.

I'd tell you more but thats all I know. I hope Julian wasn't hurt badly.

1. _____   2. _____

3. _____   4. _____

5. _____

_____

Proofread Words Circle the correct word and write it on the line.

6. Do you think **we'd   we'ld** like the movie?   6. _____

7. I **cant   can't** play right now.   7. _____

8. Before we go, **lets'   let's** say goodbye.   8. _____

9. I know **they'll   theyl'l** love this gift!   9. _____

10. He **has'nt   hasn't** found his dog yet.   10. _____

11. I think **you'll   you'l** be the winner.   11. _____

12. The team **won't   wo'nt** make the playoffs.   12. _____

School + Home **Home Activity** Your child identified misspelled contractions. Point to a spelling word. Ask your child to name the letters that were replaced by the apostrophe (').

Prefixes

Spelling Words				
unhappy	recall	disappear	unload	mistake
misspell	dislike	replace	mislead	disagree
rewrite	unroll	unknown	dishonest	react

Adding Prefixes Add a prefix to the underlined base word to make a list word. Write the list word. Read the sentence both ways.

1. Let's all help <u>load</u> the truck.
2. Our coach really knows how to <u>lead</u> the team.
3. We all <u>like</u> getting an allowance.
4. The class will <u>agree</u> with whatever you say.
5. I know I can <u>spell</u> that word.
6. You can count on that salesman to be <u>honest</u>.
7. I like to <u>write</u> letters.
8. Did you see the rabbit <u>appear</u> in the hat?

1. _____
2. _____
3. _____
4. _____
5. _____
6. _____
7. _____
8. _____

Word Meanings Write the list word that means almost the same thing as each word or phrase.

9. unfamiliar   9. _____
10. error   10. _____
11. remember   11. _____
12. spread out   12. _____
13. respond   13. _____
14. get another   14. _____
15. sad   15. _____

react
mistake
recall
unhappy
unknown
replace
unroll

School + Home **Home Activity** Your child spelled words with the prefixes *un-*, *re-*, *mis-*, and *dis-*. Point to a list word. Have your child spell the prefix and the base word separately.

Prefixes

Proofread a Letter Circle four misspelled words and write them correctly. Rewrite the second sentence, adding the missing helping verb.

Dear Mayor,

We think it's a misteak to close the swimming pool. That make alot of children unhappy. We don't dislike playgrounds, but we dissagree with changing the pool into a playground area. If you can't fix the pool, please replac it.

The Third Graders

1. _____   2. _____

3. _____   4. _____

5. _____

_____

Missing Words Fill in the circle to show the correctly spelled word. Write the word.

6. Can you _____ what we did with the flashlight?   6. _____

    ○ reacl   ○ recall   ○ ricall

7. I'll try not to _____ any words.   7. _____

    ○ misspell   ○ mispell   ○ misspel

8. Did you see that deer _____ into the woods?   8. _____

    ○ desappear   ○ disapear   ○ disappear

Home Activity Your child identified misspelled words with the prefixes *un-*, *re-*, *mis-*, and *dis-*. Name a base word. Have your child spell the list word.

Name _____

Spellings of /j/, /s/, /k/

Spelling Words				
clock	large	page	mark	kitten
judge	crack	edge	pocket	brake
change	ridge	jacket	badge	orange

Context Clues Write the missing list word. It rhymes with the underlined word.

1. The _____ wouldn't <u>budge</u> on the sentence.

2. Don't go too near the _____ of the rock <u>ledge</u>.

3. A park ranger may scratch tree <u>bark</u> to _____ a path.

4. I placed the _____ on the <u>rock</u>.

5. We used the <u>bridge</u> to cross the _____ .

6. It's <u>strange</u> that he carries so much _____ .

7. When you are ready, <u>take</u> your foot off the _____ .

8. This _____ tells how to build a <u>cage</u>.

9. The _____ likes to play with my <u>mitten</u>.

10. The old coat <u>rack</u> is starting to _____ .

11. I put my tennis <u>racket</u> under my _____ to keep it dry.

1. _____
2. _____
3. _____
4. _____
5. _____
6. _____
7. _____
8. _____
9. _____
10. _____
11. _____

Missing Words Write list words to complete the description.

The firefighter is wearing a bright (12) _____

jacket and a (13) _____ hat. He has a

(14) _____ on his (15) _____ .

School + Home **Home Activity** Your child spelled words with the consonant sounds /j/ and /k/. Ask your child to identify the letter combinations *ge*, *dge*, *ck*, and *k* in the list words.

Spellings of /j/, /s/, /k/

Proofread a Supply List Jon and Ted are organizing an overnight camping trip for the scouts. Circle four spelling mistakes. Write the words correctly. Write the item with the incorrect verb correctly.

Spelling Words
clock
large
page
mark
kitten
judge
crack
edge
pocket
brake
change
ridge
jacket
badge
orange

Bring these things:
- jackit
- raincoat or larg plastic bag
- pocket compass if you has one
- a chang of clothing
- signed permission page

Jon and I will bring are tents.

1. _____   2. _____

3. _____   4. _____

5. _____

Frequently Misspelled Words
our
I
I'm
until

Proofread Words Circle the word that is spelled correctly. Write it.

6. citten   kitten   _____

7. badg   badge   _____

8. orange   orandge   _____

9. rigde   ridge   _____

10. brake   bracke   _____

11. poket   pocket   _____

12. edge   edje   _____

© Pearson Education, Inc., 3

School + Home **Home Activity** Your child spelled words with *ge*, *dge*, *ck*, and *k*. Give clues about a list word. Have your child guess and spell the word.

Name _____

Suffixes

Spelling Words				
beautiful	safely	kindness	finally	spotless
worthless	illness	helpful	daily	suddenly
wireless	quietly	fairness	cheerful	painful

Word Endings Add an ending to the underlined word.
Then write the list word.

1. Do you floss your teeth <u>day</u>?   1. _____

2. We've <u>final</u> finished our treehouse!   2. _____

3. We sneaked <u>quiet</u> up the steps.   3. _____

4. Cell phones are <u>wire</u>.   4. _____

5. Isn't <u>fair</u> important in any game?   5. _____

6. His bicycle was <u>spot</u>.   6. _____

7. Holding the door open is a <u>help</u> thing to do.   7. _____

8. His broken leg is <u>pain</u>.   8. _____

9. Her <u>kind</u> made everyone feel better.   9. _____

10. Then <u>sudden</u> the boat turned over.   10. _____

11. She is always <u>cheer</u> when she gets up.   11. _____

Context Clues Write a list word to complete the phrase.

12. drive _____

13. _____ as a wooden nickel

14. contagious _____

15. _____ as a swan

Home Activity Your child spelled words with the suffixes *-ly*, *-ful*, *-ness*, and *-less*. Have your child pronounce each list word and identify the suffix.

Suffixes

Spelling Words				
beautiful	safely	kindness	finally	spotless
worthless	illness	helpful	daily	suddenly
wireless	quietly	fairness	cheerful	painful

Proofread a Note Christy sent a note to her neighbor who is in the hospital. Circle four spelling mistakes. Write the words correctly. Add the missing punctuation mark.

Dear Mrs Nelson,

Please get well soon! I hope your illnes is not very painful.

I've been watering your roses dayly. The yellow ones finnally bloomed. They look beautiful and very cheerfull.

Love,
Christy

Frequently Misspelled Words

finally
really

1. _____   2. _____

3. _____   4. _____

Proofread Words Fill in the circle next to the word that is spelled correctly. Write the word.

5. ○ suddennly   ○ suddenly   ○ suddenily   5. _____

6. ○ worthyles   ○ worthles   ○ worthless   6. _____

7. ○ safly   ○ safely   ○ safelly   7. _____

8. ○ quietly   ○ quietily   ○ qiuetly   8. _____

9. ○ kindnes   ○ kinness   ○ kindness   9. _____

10. ○ spotless   ○ spotles   ○ spottless   10. _____

School + Home **Home Activity** Your child spelled words with the suffixes *-ly*, *-ful*, *-ness*, and *-less.* Have your child underline the base word in each list word. Remind your child to change *i* back to *y* when necessary.

© Pearson Education, Inc., 3

Name _____

Consonant Patterns *wr, kn, gn, st, mb*

Spelling Words				
thumb	gnaw	written	know	climb
design	wrist	crumb	assign	wrench
knot	wrinkle	lamb	knob	knit

Words in Context Write the list word that completes each sentence.

1. A pup is a young dog. A _____ is a young sheep.

2. Your leg bends at the ankle. Your arm bends at the _____ .

3. You walk on a sidewalk. You _____ up a tree.

4. A bit of paper is a scrap. A bit of toast is a _____ .

5. You can weave a tablecloth. You can _____ a sweater.

6. Your big toe is on your foot. Your _____ is on your hand.

7. Music is composed. Books are _____ .

8. Chickens peck at corn. Dogs _____ on bones.

9. A carpenter uses a hammer. A plumber uses a _____ .

10. A gate has a latch. A door has a _____ .

Finishing Sentences Complete each sentence with a list word.

11. The artist painted a striped _____ on the vase.

12. I _____ how to dive.

13. He ironed every _____ out of his shirt.

14. She tied her shoelace in a _____ .

15. My teachers never _____ a lot of homework.

© Pearson Education, Inc., 3

Home Activity Your child spelled words with *wr, kn, mb,* and *gn.* Have your child pronounce each list word and identify the "silent letter" (*w* in *wr, k* in *kn, b* in *mb, g* in *gn*).

67

Consonant Patterns *wr, kn, gn, st, mb*

Proofread a Poster Circle four spelling mistakes on the poster. Write the words correctly. Then write the day and date correctly.

Art Fair!
Choose from four projects!

a. Make a wris or ankle knot bracelet.
b. Design a kite.
c. Learn an easy way to nit.
d. Make a thum puppet.

Where and wen: Room 103 on wednesday january, 15

Spelling Words
thumb
gnaw
written
know
climb
design
wrist
crumb
assign
wrench
knot
wrinkle
lamb
knob
knit

1. _____   2. _____

3. _____   4. _____

5. _____

Frequently Misspelled Words
know
when
where
what

Proofread Words Circle the correct word and write it on the line.

6. Shall we **climb** **clim** to the top of the hill?   6. _____

7. I **know** **kow** where to find the glue.   7. _____

8. The **lam** **lamb** slept by her mother.   8. _____

9. He used a **wrench** **rench** to fix the leaky pipe.   9. _____

10. Did Mr. Rice **assin** **assign** the entire page?   10. _____

11. You have a **crum** **crumb** on your chin.   11. _____

12. The mouse will **gnaw** **naw** on the wires.   12. _____

School + Home

Home Activity Your child spelled words with *wr, kn, gn, st,* and *mb*. Have your child circle these letter combinations in the list words.

Name _____

Contractions

Making Contractions Write the contraction for each pair of words.

1. will not

2. has not

3. when is

4. you will

5. he would

6. should have

7. let us

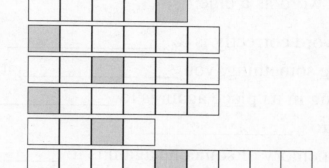

Mystery Contractions Look at the shaded boxes. Write the letters and the apostrophe to make another contraction. Then write the two words that make up the contraction.

8. _____ = _____ + _____

Contraction Equations Write a contraction by solving each math word problem. Write an apostrophe in place of the letter or letters you subtract.

9. was + not – o = _____

10. I + would – woul = _____

11. she + had – ha = _____

12. have + not – o = _____

13. can + not – no = _____

14. did + not – o = _____

15. we + had – ha = _____

© Pearson Education, Inc., 3

Home Activity Your child has been learning to spell contractions. Use a newspaper or a magazine to hunt for contractions together. See how many can be found and circled in five minutes. Work together to figure out what two words make up each contraction.

Name _____

Prefixes

Spelling Words				
unhappy	recall	disappear	unload	mistake
misspell	dislike	replace	mislead	disagree
rewrite	unroll	unknown	dishonest	react

Context Clues Write the list word that correctly completes the sentence. Use the underlined word as a clue.

1. To not <u>spell</u> a word correctly is to _____ it.

2. If you don't <u>like</u> something, you _____ it.

3. To put something in its <u>place</u> again is to _____ it.

4. To not <u>agree</u> is to _____.

5. To <u>call</u> back a memory of someone again is to _____ that person.

6. For something to <u>appear</u> and then to pass from sight is for it to _____.

7. If you <u>take</u> something the wrong way, you _____ it.

8. A person who is not <u>honest</u> is _____.

9. To <u>lead</u> someone the wrong way is to _____ that person.

10. To <u>write</u> something over is to _____ it.

11. To <u>act</u> in response to something is to _____.

Making Opposites Use the base form of a list word. Add the prefix *un-* to make a word with the opposite meaning.

known	roll	load	happy

12. Dennis will roll the towel and lay it on the sandy beach. _____

13. Lily was happy about her broken computer. _____

14. The stranger is known to me. _____

15. Please load the groceries and bring them into the house. _____

© Pearson Education, Inc., 3

Home Activity Your child has been spelling words with the prefixes *un-*, *re-*, *mis-*, and *dis-*. To practice the words together, help your child write each list word as an equation, like this: un + roll = unroll.

Spellings of /j/, /s/, /k/

Spelling Words				
clock	large	page	mark	kitten
judge	crack	edge	pocket	brake
change	ridge	jacket	badge	orange

Silly Sentences Read each silly sentence. Write the list word that rhymes with the underlined word and makes sense in the sentence.

1. I looked at a <u>sock</u> to tell the time.

1. _____

2. My <u>mitten</u> likes milk.

2. _____

3. There is a big black <u>park</u> on my paper.

3. _____

4. The <u>fudge</u> is in court right now.

4. _____

5. There is a <u>barge</u> hippo in the zoo.

5. _____

6. This book <u>stage</u> has many words on it.

6. _____

7. My <u>racket</u> has a zipper and two pockets.

7. _____

8. Dad stepped on the <u>rake</u> to stop the car.

8. _____

9. Please <u>range</u> the TV channel.

9. _____

10. I have a dime in my <u>rocket</u>.

10. _____

Letter Directions Follow each direction. Write the new word.

11. Add **ge** to **bad**.

11. _____

12. Add **o** to **range**.

12. _____

13. Subtract **pl** from **pledge**.

13. _____

14. Add **c** to **rack**.

14. _____

15. Subtract **f** from **fridge**.

15. _____

Home Activity Your child learned words spelled with *ge*, *dge*, *ck*, and *k*. To help you practice the list words with your child, say each word and ask your child to spell it. Then take turns naming words that rhyme with it.

Suffixes

Spelling Words				
beautiful	safely	kindness	finally	spotless
worthless	illness	helpful	daily	suddenly
wireless	quietly	fairness	cheerful	painful

Choosing Suffixes Circle the suffix needed to make a list word. Write the list word.

Base Word	Suffix		List Word
1. kind	ful	ness	1. _____
2. quiet	ly	ful	2. _____
3. cheer	ful	ness	3. _____
4. spot	ly	less	4. _____
5. worth	less	ful	5. _____
6. sudden	ful	ly	6. _____
7. ill	ly	ness	7. _____
8. safe	ful	ly	8. _____
9. help	ful	ness	9. _____
10. final	less	ly	10. _____

Meaning Clues Write a list word for each meaning clue.

11. full of beauty   __ __ __ __ __ __ __ __ __

12. full of pain   __ __ __ __ __ __ __

13. done each day   __ __ __ __ __

14. with no wire   __ __ __ __ __ __ __ __

Mystery Word Write the mystery word formed by the boxes. Then write the list word by adding the suffix *-ness* to the mystery word.

15. _____   _____

© Pearson Education, Inc., 3

Home Activity Your child is learning to spell words with the suffixes *-ly*, *-ful*, *-ness*, and *-less*. Help your child write list words with two different suffixes, such as *painless, painful* and *kindly, kindness*.

72

Consonant Patterns *wr, kn, gn, st, mb*

Spelling Words				
thumb	gnaw	written	know	climb
design	wrist	crumb	assign	wrench
knot	wrinkle	lamb	knob	knit

Word Search Circle the list words in the puzzle. Look across, down, and diagonally. Write the words you find.

w	r	i	n	k	l	e	b	l	c	t	f
r	g	h	k	n	o	w	x	a	m	d	n
i	p	r	q	o	c	r	u	m	b	e	w
t	s	k	v	t	h	u	m	b	t	s	r
t	w	g	n	a	w	y	k	z	b	i	e
e	d	f	c	o	h	k	p	n	v	g	n
n	c	l	i	m	b	c	x	a	i	n	c
a	s	s	i	g	n	w	r	i	s	t	h

1. _____   6. _____   11. _____
2. _____   7. _____   12. _____
3. _____   8. _____   13. _____
4. _____   9. _____   14. _____
5. _____   10. _____   15. _____

Home Activity Your child practiced spelling words with *wr, kn, gn, st,* and *mb*. Ask your child to write each list word. Have him or her underline the *wr, kn, gn, st,* and *mb* in each word and to X out the letter in each pair that is silent.

Irregular Plurals

Spelling Words				
wolves	knives	feet	men	children
women	sheep	heroes	scarves	mice
geese	cuffs	elves	banjos	halves

Seeing Relationships Write list words to complete the comparisons.

1. arms and hands, legs and _____

2. cats and lions, dogs and _____

3. feet and shoes, necks and _____

4. milk and cows, wool and _____

5. boys and girls, men and _____

6. tubas and trumpets, violins and _____

7. grown and adults, young and _____

8. fur and rabbits, feathers and _____

9. leaders and followers, cowards and _____

10. four and fourths, two and _____

1. _____

2. _____

3. _____

4. _____

5. _____

6. _____

7. _____

8. _____

9. _____

10. _____

Rhyming Plurals Write a list word that rhymes with the underlined word.

11. The _____ on my coat look like <u>puffs</u> of fur.

12. The _____ in this story live on toy <u>shelves</u>.

13. We've found _____ in the garage <u>twice</u>.

14. The _____ put the cattle back in the <u>pen</u>.

15. They carry _____ on <u>dives</u> in dangerous water.

11. _____

12. _____

13. _____

14. _____

15. _____

© Pearson Education, Inc., 3

School + Home **Home Activity** Your child spelled plural words. Name a list word. Ask your child to explain how the plural was formed.

Name _____

Irregular Plurals

Proofread a Report Robbie wrote a report about the class field trip. Circle four misspelled words. Write them correctly. Write the verb Robbie should have used in his second sentence.

> Our class went to the nature center. We seen sheep, gese, and even some wolves.
>
> The two wemen who showed us around said wolves eat everything from big deer to little field mouses—but not children! Still, I wouldn't wunt to get too close to a wolf.

1. _____
2. _____
3. _____
4. _____
5. _____

Spelling Words

- wolves
- knives
- feet
- men
- children
- women
- sheep
- heroes

- scarves
- mice
- geese
- cuffs
- elves
- banjos
- halves

Frequently Misspelled Words

- clothes
- want

Proofread Words Fill in a circle to show which word is spelled correctly. Write the word.

6. Two musicians played _____ for the square dance.
   ○ banjoes   ○ banjos   ○ banjoys

   6. _____

7. We rolled up our _____ and went to work.
   ○ cuves   ○ cuffes   ○ cuffs

   7. _____

8. The _____ helped the shoemaker with his work.
   ○ elves   ○ elfs   ○ elvies

   8. _____

9. My mom has some pretty _____ .
   ○ scarves   ○ scarfs   ○ scarvs

   9. _____

10. The police officers were _____ .
    ○ herros   ○ heroes   ○ heros

    10. _____

Home Activity Your child identified misspelled plurals. Say the singular form of a list word. Ask your child to spell the plural.

© Pearson Education, Inc., 3

75

Name _____

Vowels: *r*-Controlled

Spelling Words				
third	early	world	certain	dirty
herself	earth	word	perfect	verb
nerve	worm	thirsty	workout	earn

Complete the Sentence Write a list word to complete the sentence.

1. This is really a _____ day!

1. _____

2. He had a _____ at the gym.

2. _____

3. I put a _____ on my fishhook.

3. _____

4. May I have a _____ with you?

4. _____

5. I'm so _____ I could drink a gallon of water!

5. _____

6. Don't lose your _____!

6. _____

7. I'd like to travel around the _____ .

7. _____

8. This is the _____ time we've won.

8. _____

Opposites Write a list word that means the opposite.

9. late

9. _____

10. unsure

10. _____

11. noun

11. _____

12. himself

12. _____

13. sky

13. _____

14. clean

14. _____

15. win

15. _____

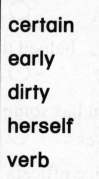

earth
certain
early
dirty
herself
verb
earn

© Pearson Education, Inc., 3

School + Home **Home Activity** Your child spelled words with *er*, *ir*, *or*, and *ear*. Have your child circle these letter combinations in the list words.

Vowels: *r*-Controlled

Proofread Workout Tips Circle four misspelled words. Write them correctly. Cross out the incorrect end mark and write the correct one.

> Workout Tips
> • Some people plan a workout early in the day, but there's no pirfect time. Just be ceartain you do it!
> • Drink extra water—even if you're not thersty.
> • Do something you like. Have you herd that jogging is best.

1. _____ 2. _____

3. _____ 4. _____

Proofread Words Circle the correctly spelled word. Write it.

5. nurve   nerve   5. _____

6. worm   werm   6. _____

7. ern   earn   7. _____

8. dirty   durty   8. _____

9. third   therd   9. _____

10. hurself   herself   10. _____

11. workout   werkout   11. _____

12. vurb   verb   12. _____

© Pearson Education, Inc., 3

Home Activity Your child identified misspelled words with *er*, *ir*, *or*, and *ear*. Pronounce a word. Ask your child to tell which letter combination it contains—*er*, *ir*, *or*, or *ear*.

Name _____

Prefixes

Context Clues Write a list word that best completes each sentence.

1. Dad had to work _____ .

2. He stayed up until _____ .

3. The sink began to _____ .

4. My uncle is flying to the _____ .

5. The word *midpoint* has a _____ .

6. My sister is _____ .

7. Before you begin your report, make an _____ .

8. The shrubs look _____ .

9. Our teacher had us take a _____ .

10. My library book is _____ .

Missing Prefixes Write the prefix. Write the list word.

11. _____ doors   11. _____

12. _____ point   12. _____

13. _____ paid   13. _____

14. _____ side   14. _____

15. _____ field   15. _____

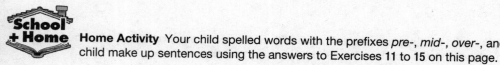

Prefixes

Proofread an Announcement Circle four misspelled
words. Write them correctly. Rewrite the sentence that
has an incorrect verb.

Spelling Words

prepaid
midnight
overflow
outdoors
outline
overgrown
prefix
Midwest

pretest
midpoint
outgoing
overtime
overdue
outside
outfield

Night Hike

Learn about creatures of the night!

Meet outside the nature center. Dress for
outdores and wear long pants. Some areas
is overgroan.

8 P.M. to mid night
Bring a freind!

Note: The $2 fee must be prepaid.

---

1. _____   2. _____

3. _____   4. _____

5. _____

**Frequently
Misspelled
Words**

outside
friend

Proofread Words Fill in a circle to show which word
is spelled correctly. Write the word.

6. ○ middwest   ○ Midwest   ○ midWest   _____
7. ○ overfloe   ○ overflow   ○ ovrflow   _____
8. ○ outgoing   ○ ootgoing   ○ outtgoing   _____
9. ○ midpoin   ○ midpointe   ○ midpoint   _____
10. ○ outfield   ○ outfeild   ○ outfeeled   _____
11. ○ pritest   ○ pretest   ○ preetest   _____
12. ○ ovrtime   ○ overrtime   ○ overtime   _____

© Pearson Education, Inc., 3

School + Home **Home Activity** Your child identified misspelled words with the prefixes *pre-*, *mid-*, *over-*,
and *out-*. Pronounce a word. Ask your child to identify the prefix and spell the word.

Suffixes

Spelling Words				
dentist	editor	artist	hostess	actress
swimmer	seller	tutor	tourist	organist
lioness	shipper	chemist	investor	conductor

Definitions Write a list word to name each person.

1. a person who draws and paints   1. _____

2. a person who takes care of teeth   2. _____

3. a person who moves through water   3. _____

4. a person who receives guests   4. _____

5. a person who teaches   5. _____

6. a person who works on books or magazines 6. _____

7. a person who buys and sells stocks   7. _____

8. a person who leads an orchestra   8. _____

9. a person who plays an organ   9. _____

10. a person who works with chemicals   10. _____

11. a person who travels to new places   11. _____

Rhymes Write the missing word. It rhymes with the underlined word.

12. The _____ sent my sweater in a <u>zipper</u> bag.   12. _____

13. He got a <u>propeller</u> from a model plane _____.   13. _____

14. Did you see the <u>mess</u> the _____ left backstage? 14. _____

15. The _____ eats <u>less</u> food than the lion.   15. _____

Home Activity Your child spelled words with the suffixes *-er*, *-or*, *-ess*, and *-ist*. Many of the list words refer to people or occupations. Discuss any unfamiliar words with your child.

Name _____

Suffixes

Spelling Words				
dentist	editor	artist	hostess	actress
swimmer	seller	tutor	tourist	organist
lioness	shipper	chemist	investor	conductor

Proofread a Program Nick wrote the program for the school musical. Circle four misspelled words. Write them correctly. Add the missing punctuation mark.

The Cast

Mad chemist....Don Perlas

The dentest......Julie Blake

The tourist.......Kate Hanson

Music conducter....Steve Carr

Scenery artist....Ann Morgan

We extend special thanks to the editer of the *Daily Press*, Mr Pearson, hoo is our sponsor.

Frequently Misspelled Words

once
who
one

1. _____

2. _____

3. _____

4. _____

Proofread Words Circle the word that is spelled correctly. Write the word.

5. Jake was a ticket **seller   sellor**.

6. A **tudor   tutor**   helps Don with math.

7. Jean is a fast **swimmer   swimer**.

8. The **organist   organest**   played softly.

9. We thanked our **hostes   hostess**.

10. The **lioness   liones**   paced back and forth.

5. _____

6. _____

7. _____

8. _____

9. _____

10. _____

Home Activity Your child identified misspelled words with the suffixes *-er*, *-or*, *-ess*, and *-ist*. Ask your child to name the four hardest words. Have your child write these words.

Name _____

Syllables VCCCV

Spelling Words				
monster	surprise	hundred	complete	control
sample	instant	inspect	pilgrim	contrast
explode	district	address	substance	children

Missing Words Write the missing list word to complete each sentence.

1. That was a _____!

2. Would you like a _____ of lime yogurt?

3. That balloon will _____ if you keep blowing.

4. The _____ went on a long journey.

5. I couldn't _____ my tears.

6. My little sister thinks a _____ lives under her bed.

7. Many officials _____ the coal mine every year.

8. My best friend is not in my school _____.

1. _____

2. _____

3. _____

4. _____

5. _____

6. _____

7. _____

8. _____

Definitions Write the list word that means the same thing as the word or phrase.

9. one more than ninety-nine

10. many boys and girls

11. entire

12. material

13. difference

14. moment of time

15. numbers that tell where you live

9. _____

10. _____

11. _____

12. _____

13. _____

14. _____

15. _____

© Pearson Education, Inc., 3

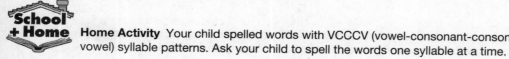

School + Home **Home Activity** Your child spelled words with VCCCV (vowel-consonant-consonant-consonant-vowel) syllable patterns. Ask your child to spell the words one syllable at a time.

82

Syllables VCCCV

Spelling Words				
monster	surprise	hundred	complete	control
sample	instant	inspect	pilgrim	contrast
explode	district	address	substance	children

Proofread a Paragraph James wrote about stamp collecting. Circle four words that are spelled incorrectly. Cross out the extra word in the first sentence.

Some childrn try to collect a sample of each stamp pictured over in a stamp album. I tried that, but I thought I'd never get a complete collection. Most of my pages were empty. Now I collect only Chrismas stamps. I have almost two hunderd stamps. Does that surpris you?

Frequently Misspelled Words

Christmas
went

1. _____ 2. _____

3. _____ 4. _____

Proofread Words Fill in a circle to show which word is spelled correctly. Write the word.

5. In the dark, the tree looked like a _____ .
   ○ monstor   ○ monster   ○ montser

5. _____

6. They gave me a free _____ at the grocery store.
   ○ sample   ○ saple   ○ slampe

6. _____

7. What is your _____ ?
   ○ adress   ○ addres   ○ address

7. _____

8. I ate so much, I thought I would _____ !
   ○ explod   ○ esplode   ○ explode

8. _____

School + Home **Home Activity** Your child spelled words with VCCCV (vowel-consonant-consonant-consonant-vowel) syllable patterns. Have your child circle the three consecutive consonants in a list word and underline the vowels on either side.

© Pearson Education, Inc., 3

Irregular Plurals

Spelling Words				
wolves	knives	feet	men	children
women	sheep	heroes	scarves	mice
geese	cuffs	elves	banjos	halves

Word Meanings Write the list word for each meaning clue.

1. animals that give wool

2. more than one mouse

3. stringed instruments

4. brave people

5. two equal parts of a whole

6. more than one man

7. small make-believe people

Complete the Sentence Write the letters from the shaded boxes to finish the sentence.

8. People wear _____ around their necks.

Proofreading Draw a line through the misspelled word in each sentence. Write the word correctly.

9. The childrun learned spelling words. _____

10. The wolfs howled at the moon. _____

11. A baby has small foots. _____

12. A flock of gooses flew over us. _____

13. I got mustard on my shirt cuffes. _____

14. These knifes are very sharp. _____

15. Three womin painted the room. _____

 Home Activity Your child is learning to spell irregular plurals. Say the singular form of a list word (*mouse*). Ask your child to spell the plural (*mice*). Continue until all the words have been spelled.

Name _____

Vowels: *r*-Controlled

Spelling Words				
third	early	world	certain	dirty
herself	earth	word	perfect	verb
nerve	worm	thirsty	workout	earn

Classifying Write the list word that belongs in each group.

1. first, second, ___

2. yourself, himself, ___

3. letter, syllable, ___

4. unclean, messy, ___

5. positive, sure, ___

6. correct, all right, ___

7. noun, adjective, ___

1. _____

2. _____

3. _____

4. _____

5. _____

6. _____

7. _____

Scrambled Words Unscramble the list words. Write them correctly.

8. lyear

9. enrve

10. hirstyt

11. touwkor

12. nrea

13. threa

14. rowld

15. rowm

8. __ __ __ __ __

9. __ __ __ __ __

10. __ __ __ __ __ __ __

11. __ __ __ __ __ __ __

12. __ __ __ __

13. __ __ __ __ __

14. __ __ __ __ __

15. __ __ __ __

Proverb Write the words you wrote for number 8 and for number 15. You will read some famous words of wisdom.

The _____ bird catches the _____ .
    8   15

© Pearson Education, Inc., 3

Home Activity Your child practiced spelling words with *er*, *ir*, *or*, and *ear*. Ask your child to write the words and to circle the letters for the *r*-vowel sounds. Then read the words together. When you come to circled letters, exaggerate the vowel sound by stretching it out.

85

Name _____

Prefixes

Opposites Write the list word that is opposite in meaning to the given word or phrase.

1. indoors _____
2. suffix _____
3. noon _____
4. on time _____
5. posttest _____
6. infield _____
7. Mideast _____
8. inside _____

Spelling Words

prepaid
midnight
overflow
outdoors
outline
overgrown
prefix
Midwest

pretest
midpoint
outgoing
overtime
overdue
outside
outfield

Word Search Circle the list words in the puzzle. Look across and down. Write the words you find.

m	o	u	t	g	o	i	n	g	a	c
i	v	o	v	e	r	g	r	o	w	n
d	e	v	f	g	m	s	w	u	g	l
p	r	e	p	a	i	d	t	t	p	s
o	f	v	m	u	n	y	r	l	w	a
i	l	t	o	v	e	r	t	i	m	e
n	o	q	b	f	v	p	c	n	l	b
t	w	s	k	i	z	g	v	e	u	m

9. _____   12. _____   14. _____
10. _____   13. _____   15. _____
11. _____

Home Activity Your child learned to spell words with the prefixes *pre-*, *mid-*, *over-*, and *out-*. Make two sets of cards with list words on them. Play Concentration. When a match is made, the person must spell the word correctly to keep the cards.

© Pearson Education, Inc., 3

Name _____

Suffixes

Spelling Words				
dentist	editor	artist	hostess	actress
swimmer	seller	tutor	tourist	organist
lioness	shipper	chemist	investor	conductor

Adding Suffixes Add a suffix to the base word. Write the list word you make in the chart.

base	-er	-or	-ess	-ist
1. invest				
2. tour				
3. sell				
4. lion				
5. art				
6. edit				
7. host				
8. organ				
9. conduct				

Proofreading Circle the correctly spelled word. Write the word.

10. dentalist   dentist   **11.** _____

11. actess   actress   **11.** _____

12. shipper   shiper   **12.** _____

13. tutor   tuter   **13.** _____

14. swimer   swimmer   **14.** _____

15. chemist   chemest   **15.** _____

Home Activity Your child practiced spelling words with the suffixes *-er*, *-or*, *-ess*, and *-ist*. To practice together, choose a word. Draw blanks for each letter, then write in the suffix. Let your child guess the word and fill in the remaining blanks. Then have him or her write the whole word.

Name _____

Syllables VCCCV

Spelling Words				
monster	surprise	hundred	complete	control
sample	instant	inspect	pilgrim	contrast
explode	district	address	substance	children

Analogies Write the list word that completes each comparison.

1. **Adult** is to **adults** as **child** is to _____.

2. **Begin** is to **end** as **unfinished** is to _____.

3. **1,000** is to **thousand** as **100** is to _____.

4. **Check** is to **examine** as **examine** is to _____.

5. **Light** is to **dark** as **compare** is to _____.

6. **Quick** is to **fast** as **immediate** is to _____.

7. **Explorer** is to **pioneer** as **traveler** is to _____.

8. **Real** is to **person** as **make-believe** is to _____.

Finding Syllables Decide where to divide each word into syllables.
Write each syllable. Remember that for VCCCV words, you divide after
the first consonant.

hundred = hun dred

9. surprise _____ _____

10. control _____ _____

11. sample _____ _____

12. substance _____ _____

13. address _____ _____

14. district _____ _____

15. explode _____ _____

Home Activity Your child is learning spelling words with the VCCCV (vowel-consonant-
consonant-consonant-vowel) syllable pattern. Ask your child to write each word and to circle in
crayon the three consonants that come together.

Name _____

Syllable Pattern CV/VC

Spelling Words				
create	medium	piano	idea	radio
video	studio	violin	duo	patio
rodeo	pioneer	trio	stadium	audio

Connections Connect the first and last parts of the word.
Write the word.

vide-	-oneer	1. _____
vi-	-o	2. _____
pi-	-um	3. _____
stadi-	-a	4. _____
ide-	-olin	5. _____

Seeing Relationships Read the first word pair. Write a list word to
complete the second word pair.

6. see and television, hear and _____   6. _____

7. farmer and field, artist and _____   7. _____

8. huge and large, middle-sized and _____   8. _____

9. ceiling and dining room, sky and _____   9. _____

10. three and trio, two and _____   10. _____

11. wreck and fix, destroy and _____   11. _____

12. sight and video, sound and _____   12. _____

13. clang and bell, music and _____   13. _____

14. twin and duo, triplet and _____   14. _____

15. clown and circus, cowboy and _____   15. _____

© Pearson Education, Inc., 3

Home Activity Your child spelled words with CV/VC (consonant-vowel-vowel-consonant) syllable
pattern. Discuss any list words that may be unfamiliar to your child.

Name _____

Syllable Pattern CV/VC

Proofread a Menu Circle four misspelled words in the menu specials. Write them correctly. Write an adjective that could have been used instead of *nice*.

Spelling Words

create
medium
piano
idea
radio
video
studio
violin

duo
patio
rodeo
pioneer
trio
stadium
audio

Pioneer Cáfe

Specials

Lunch duo.......1/2 sandwich, soup of the day
Lunch treo.......1/2 sandwich, soup of the day,
            salad

Our favorite float: a meduim cola with berry
            ice cream
You won't beleive how good it is!
Or, creat your own nice float flavor.

Frequently Misspelled Words

cousin
believe

---

1. _____ 2. _____

3. _____ 4. _____

5. _____

Proofread Words Circle the word that is spelled correctly. Write it on the line.

6. Did you see the new **stadium   staduim**? 6. _____

7. We watched a **vidio   video** last night. 7. _____

8. Tara plays the **paino   piano**. 8. _____

9. Your **idia   idea** is fantastic! 9. _____

10. I like that **radio   radioe** station! 10. _____

© Pearson Education, Inc., 3

School + Home **Home Activity** Your child spelled words with CVVC (consonant-vowel-vowel-consonant) and CVV (consonant-vowel-vowel) syllable patterns. Have your child divide the list words into syllables.

90

Name _____

Homophones

Spelling Words				
to	too	two	week	weak
road	rode	stair	stare	bear
bare	write	right	new	knew

Context Clues Write the missing words. Use all the words in each homophone group in one sentence.

Do you (1) _____ with your (2) _____ hand?

1. _____   2. _____

The (3) _____ dogs want (4) _____ eat (5) _____ .

3. _____   4. _____   5. _____

Sam (6) _____ he'd get a (7) _____ bike.

6. _____   7. _____

We (8) _____ on the bumpy (9) _____.

8. _____   9. _____

He's felt (10) _____ all (11) _____ .

10. _____   11. _____

The dancing (12) _____ danced in its (13) _____ feet.

12. _____   13. _____

The cats just (14) _____ at the (15) _____ .

14. _____   15. _____ .

© Pearson Education, Inc., 3

Home Activity Your child wrote homophones. Point to a list word. Have your child use the word in a sentence.

Name _____

Homophones

Proofread Directions Becky wrote directions to her house. Circle four misspelled words. Write them correctly. What word should Becky have used instead of **shortest**? Write it.

- • Start on Sunshine Rode
- • Go to the flower shop.
- • Turn write after two blocks.
- • It's across from the knew park.
- • There are too yellow houses. It's the shortest one.

1. _____

2. _____

3. _____

4. _____

5. _____

Frequently Misspelled Words

too

two

Meaning Connections Write a list word to complete the sentence.

6. I'm the art helper this _____ .

7. It's a grizzly _____ !

8. Mom _____ the train to work.

9. We just _____ the boat would sink.

10. The box is on the top _____ .

11. Tie the leash _____ the post.

12. Don't use _____ much flour in the cake.

6. _____

7. _____

8. _____

9. _____

10. _____

11. _____

12. _____

© Pearson Education, Inc., 3

School + Home **Home Activity** Your child identified misspelled homophones. Ask your child to spell and define three groups of homophones.

Vowel Patterns *au, augh, ou, ough*

Spelling Words				
because	though	taught	bought	touch
would	author	could	enough	sausage
fought	should	faucet	daughter	brought

Definitions Write the list word that fits the clue.

1. gave instructions
2. battled for something
3. writer of articles or stories
4. opposite of the word *son*
5. paid for something

1. _____
2. _____
3. _____
4. _____
5. _____

Word Meanings Write the missing list word to complete each sentence.

6. Anjay likes cheese and _____ on his crackers.
7. We _____ not swim after eating.
8. My mom made _____ salad for ten people.
9. We won the game _____ of good defense.
10. Andrea got water from the _____.
11. On Fitness Day, I _____ a jump rope to school.
12. The blanket is soft to _____.
13. If we practice, we _____ be great.
14. We need the key to get inside, _____.
15. I _____ love to watch that program!

6. _____
7. _____
8. _____
9. _____
10. _____
11. _____
12. _____
13. _____
14. _____
15. _____

© Pearson Education, Inc., 3

Home Activity Your child wrote words with *au, augh, ou,* and *ough* that make different vowel sounds. Have your child pronounce each word to make sure they are saying the vowel sound correctly.

Name _____

Vowel Patterns *au, augh, ou, ough*

Spelling Words				
because	though	taught	bought	touch
would	author	could	enough	sausage
fought	should	faucet	daughter	brought

Proofread a List Ella wrote about her day in class. Circle the four spelling mistakes. Write the words correctly. Write the word Ella should have used in the last sentence instead of better.

Class was very interesting becauze we had a guest speaker. She was an author. She brout her book with her. The book was about goals. She said we shoold always have goals. She tawt us to aim high and be the better we can be.

1. _____

2. _____

3. _____

4. _____

5. _____

Frequently Misspelled Words

because
caught
thought

Proofread Words Fill in a circle to show which word is spelled correctly. Write the word.

6. ○ fout   ○ fawt   ○ fought   _____

7. ○ faucet   ○ fawcet   ○ foucet   _____

8. ○ tuch   ○ touch   ○ toucgh   _____

9. ○ enuff   ○ enouh   ○ enough   _____

10. ○ woud   ○ would   ○ woughd   _____

11. ○ could   ○ cood   ○ coud   _____

12. ○ thogh   ○ thow   ○ though   _____

Home Activity Your child wrote words with *au, augh, ou,* and *ough* that make different vowel sounds. Ask your child to circle the four hardest words for him or her to spell and then write them.

Name _____

Vowel Patterns *ei, eigh*

Spelling Words				
ceiling	neighbor	either	eighteen	height
neither	weight	leisure	protein	freight
receive	weigh	deceive	sleigh	conceited

Finish the Sentence Write a list word to complete the sentence.

1. How much does the bag _____?   1. _____

2. I want to go for a _____ ride.   2. _____

3. My _____ is moving soon.   3. _____

4. Meat is a good source of _____.   4. _____

5. I want _____ soup or salad.   5. _____

6. My cousin is _____ years old.   6. _____

7. The _____ of the bridge is 150 feet.   7. _____

8. The train was loaded with _____.   8. _____

9. The _____ was too heavy for me to lift.   9. _____

Definitions Write the list word that fits the clue.

10. time to rest and play   10. _____

11. opposite of the word *give*   11. _____

12. rhymes with the word *greeted*   12. _____

13. to try to trick   13. _____

14. rhymes with the word *either*   14. _____

15. opposite of the word *floor*   15. _____

| neither |
| leisure |
| ceiling |
| receive |
| deceive |
| conceited |

© Pearson Education, Inc., 3

Home Activity Your child wrote words with the vowel pattern *ei* and *eigh*. Read a sentence on this page. Ask your child to spell the list word.

Name _____

Vowel Patterns *ei, eigh*

Spelling Words				
ceiling	neighbor	either	eighteen	height
neither	weight	leisure	protein	freight
receive	weigh	deceive	sleigh	conceited

Proofread a Paragraph Jay wrote his opinion about the best breed of dog. Circle the four misspelled words. Write them correctly. Then rewrite the run-on sentence as two separate sentences.

I think the labrador is the best dog. They are eether black, chocolate, or yellow. They are very friendly with family, naybors, and even the mailman! They wiegh a lot, so you have to make sure they don't sit on you, if they do you might get licked. There is allmost nothing you can't do with a labrador!

Frequently Misspelled Words

believe
friend

1. _____   2. _____

3. _____   4. _____

5. _____

Proofread Words Circle the word that is spelled correctly. Write it.

6. ceiling   cieling   6. _____

7. neether   neither   7. _____

8. eightteen   eighteen   8. _____

9. height   hight   9. _____

10. protein   proteine   10. _____

11. sleigh   sleiy   11. _____

12. decieve   deceive   12. _____

School + Home **Home Activity** Your child identified misspelled words with the vowel pattern *ei* and *eigh*. Have your child pronounce each spelling word and underline the vowel patterns.

© Pearson Education, Inc., 3

Suffixes

Spelling Words				
rocky	foolish	rainy	childhood	selfish
treatment	movement	neighborhood	childish	parenthood
crunchy	bumpy	payment	sleepy	shipment

Opposites Write the missing list word. It will be the **opposite** of the underlined word.

1. This lizard's skin is <u>smooth</u>.

2. Do you think tomorrow will be <u>sunny</u>?

3. I was <u>alert</u> the entire trip.

4. The salesman was <u>generous</u> with his time.

5. There's a lot of <u>stillness</u> in the wasp nest.

6. Our guide seemed <u>wise</u> to me.

7. My brother acts pretty <u>grown up</u>.

8. Dad collected coins throughout his <u>adulthood</u>.

1. _____

2. _____

3. _____

4. _____

5. _____

6. _____

7. _____

8. _____

Context Clues A word is missing from each of the opinions below. Write the missing word.

9. Jelly with _____ peanut butter tastes best.

10. Anyone would like to get a _____ of gifts.

11. I should get a _____ for washing dishes.

12. My _____ is the friendliest.

13. A _____ beach is not much fun.

14. There's nothing easy about _____ .

15. The best _____ for a cold is to rest.

Home Activity Your child spelled words with the suffixes *-y*, *-ish*, *-hood*, and *-ment*. Have your child try spelling the base word and the suffix separately.

Suffixes

Name _____

Spelling Words				
rocky	foolish	rainy	childhood	selfish
treatment	movement	neighborhood	childish	parenthood
crunchy	bumpy	payment	sleepy	shipment

Proofread an Order Form Greg is selling snack bars for his team. Circle four spelling errors and one capitalization error. Write the words correctly.

Order Form		
Item	**How Many?**	**Cost**
rocky road bars	3	$ 3.00
crunchie bars	2	$ 2.00
	Total:	$ 5.00

Deliver to: 1413 Sleepy Hollow Road

Notes: Deliver on saturday.
Leave the box on the vary top step unless it is rainey.
The paymant has been made.

Frequently Misspelled Words
different
very

1. _____   2. _____   3. _____

4. _____   5. _____

Proofread Words Circle the word that is spelled correctly.

6. The **shipmint   shipment** should arrive soon.

7. This ride is **bumpy   bumpie**.

8. Don't be **selfist   selfish** with the markers.

9. We are having a **nieghborhood   neighborhood** picnic.

10. He spent his **childhood   childood** in Cleveland.

Home Activity Your child identified misspelled words with the suffixes -y, -ish, -hood, and -ment. Have your child underline the suffixes in the list words.

Name _____

Syllable Pattern CV/VC

Spelling Words				
create	medium	piano	idea	radio
video	studio	violin	duo	patio
rodeo	pioneer	trio	stadium	audio

Hidden Words Circle the list word hidden in each puzzle. Write the word.

1. m b c r e a t e t c   _____
2. c p i o n e e r d g   _____
3. b n k m e d i u m   _____
4. f o i d e a j d c a   _____
5. o l s t a d i u m   _____
6. u v i o l i n l m p   _____

Meaning Clues Circle the word that fits the meaning clue. Write it.

7. moving pictures   video or audio   _____
8. outdoor space   piano or patio   _____
9. pair   duo or radio   _____
10. artist's workplace   rodeo or studio   _____
11. sound   audio or duo   _____
12. group of three   trio or duo   _____
13. hear music and news here   patio or radio   _____
14. instrument with keys   piano or radio   _____
15. place where cowboys compete   radio or rodeo   _____

Summarizing Look at the words you wrote for numbers 7–15. Write a sentence that tells how they are all alike.

_____

Home Activity Your child spelled words with the CVVC (consonant-vowel-vowel-consonant) and CVV (consonant-vowel-vowel) syllable patterns. Together, write the words on a calendar page. Fill the calendar. Take turns choosing a date and spelling the word on that date.

Name _____

Homophones

Spelling Words				
to	too	two	week	weak
road	rode	stair	stare	bear
bare	write	right	new	knew

Complete the Sentences Write the list word that completes each sentence.

1. Jason has (to, two) bikes. _____

2. Next (week, weak) is my eighth birthday. _____

3. Can you (write, right) neatly with a pen? _____

4. Do not (stair, stare) at people on the street. _____

5. Maya wants to go to the party (two, too). _____

6. Which (road, rode) goes to the park? _____

7. Maya had no shoes, so her feet were (bear, bare). _____

8. Who (new, knew) the answer to the problem? _____

9. I tripped on a (stair, stare) and fell. _____

Mixed-up Homophones Cross out two incorrectly used list words in each sentence. Write the correct words.

A knew baby kitten is very week.

10. _____   11. _____

We road too the show in a big car.

12. _____   13. _____

Is the bare in the write cage?

14. _____   15. _____

© Pearson Education, Inc., 3

 Home Activity Your child is learning to spell homophones—words with the same pronunciation but different spellings and meanings. Ask your child to point to a list word, spell it, and use it in a sentence. Continue until all words have been used.

Vowel Patterns *au, augh, ou, ough*

Spelling Words

because	though	taught	bought	touch
would	author	could	enough	sausage
fought	should	faucet	daughter	brought

Synonyms Write the list word for each synonym or synonym phrase. The answer to the riddle will be in the shaded boxes.

What is a skunk worth?

1. writer
2. meat
3. able to
4. female child
5. all that was needed
6. water tap

Before and After Write the list word that begins and ends with the same letters as each word shown.

7. bright _____
8. bone _____
9. world _____
10. said _____
11. trench _____
12. alter _____

School + Home **Home Activity** Your child is learning to spell words with *au, augh, ou,* and *ough*. Ask your child to circle these letters in each word and say the vowel sound that each makes.

Vowel Patterns *ei, eigh*

Spelling Words				
ceiling	neighbor	either	eighteen	height
neither	weight	leisure	protein	freight
receive	weigh	deceive	sleigh	conceited

Crossword Puzzle Write the list word that could be used in an answer to each question.

Across

2. the top of a room

5. how tall something is

6. cargo

7. trick

Down

1. to get

2. overly proud

3. not either

4. carriage used on snow

Alphabetizing Write each group of words in ABC order.

neighbor
protein
either

9. _____

10. _____

11. _____

weight
leisure
eighteen

12. _____

13. _____

14. _____

© Pearson Education, Inc., 3

School + Home **Home Activity** Your child learned spelling words with the vowel pattern *ei* and *eigh*. Together, divide the words into two groups based on their vowel pattern. Ask your child to choose words from each group to spell to you.

Name _____

Suffixes

Spelling Words

rocky	foolish	rainy	childhood	selfish
treatment	movement	neighborhood	childish	parenthood
crunchy	bumpy	payment	sleepy	shipment

Suffix Story Read the story. Circle each list word where the writer forgot to use a suffix. Write the word with its suffix.

One rain day a fool king went for a ride.

1. _____   2. _____

The road was bump and rock.

3. _____   4. _____

The king wanted to get a ship of crunch cereal.

5. _____   6. _____

The move of the coach made the king feel sleep.

7. _____   8. _____

In the right neighbor, the king made a pay for the cereal.

9. _____   10. _____

The self king was very child and gobbled up all the cereal with both hands.

11. _____   12. _____

This was his treat of cereal ever since child.

13. _____   14. _____

Parent should help him know better.

15. _____

Home Activity Your child spelled words with the suffixes *-y*, *-ish*, *-hood*, and *-ment*. Have your child read the story on the page, using the words he or she wrote as answers.

Name _____

Vowel Sounds in *moon* and *foot*

Names Write list words to name the pictures.

1. _____ 2. _____ 3. _____

Categorizing Add a list word to each group.

4. duck, chicken, ___   4. _____

5. cake, pie, ___   5. _____

6. paste, tape, ___   6. _____

7. Sunday, Thursday, ___   7. _____

8. pillow, pad, ___   8. _____

9. liter, quart, ___   9. _____

Rhyming Words Complete each sentence with a list word that rhymes with the underlined word.

10. We <u>grew</u> a _____ different kinds of vegetables.

11. It's _____ that <u>blue</u> is my favorite color.

12. I will blow up your _____ <u>soon</u>.

13. The meat in this <u>stew</u> is hard to _____ .

14. That <u>doodle</u> you drew looks like a _____ .

15. The _____ building seems <u>cool</u> today.

Home Activity Your child wrote words with the vowel sound in *moon* (spelled *oo, ew, ue, ui*) and the vowel sound in *foot* (spelled *oo, u*). Have your child pronounce and spell the words with *oo*.

School + Home

Name _____

Vowel Sounds in *moon* and *foot*

Spelling Words				
few	school	true	goose	fruit
cookie	cushion	noodle	bookmark	balloon
suit	chew	glue	Tuesday	bushel

Proofread a Schedule Kelsey made a schedule. Circle four spelling errors on this week's page. Write the words correctly. Then circle five words that need capital letters.

monday	no school—cuold go to Gym for Kids
tuesday	fruit and cooky sale
wednesday	blow up ballons for party
thursday	Jena's birthday party
friday	Jena's tru birthday

Frequently Misspelled Words

through
took
would
could

1. _____ 2. _____

3. _____ 4. _____

Proofread Words Fill in a circle to show which word is spelled correctly. Write it.

5. ○ noddle ○ noodle ○ noodel 5. _____

6. ○ bookmark ○ bukmark ○ book mark 6. _____

7. ○ cushon ○ cushion ○ cooshion 7. _____

8. ○ ballewn ○ ballon ○ balloon 8. _____

9. ○ glew ○ gleu ○ glue 9. _____

10. ○ friut ○ fruit ○ froot 10. _____

© Pearson Education, Inc., 3

Home Activity Your child identified misspelled words with the vowel sound in *moon* (spelled *oo, ew, ue, ui*) and the vowel sound in *foot* (spelled *oo, u*). Ask your child to write a sentence containing two or more list words.

105

Name _____

Schwa

Spelling Words				
above	another	upon	animal	paper
open	family	travel	afraid	nickel
sugar	circus	item	gallon	melon

Context Clues Write the missing spelling word.

1. May I have _____ piece of pizza?

2. I have three dimes and one _____ in my bank.

3. He was eating a slice of _____.

4. I wrote a letter on a sheet of green _____.

5. My _____ likes to watch football Sunday afternoons.

6. Please get a _____ of milk.

7. The _____ had clowns and acrobats.

8. Is the _____ bowl empty?

9. Each _____ on the list must be done by noon.

10. Once _____ a time, there was a handsome prince.

11. My favorite _____ is the giraffe.

1. _____

2. _____

3. _____

4. _____

5. _____

6. _____

7. _____

8. _____

9. _____

10. _____

11. _____

Opposites Write the spelling word that means the opposite.

12. shut   _____

13. brave   _____

14. stay home   _____

15. below   _____

| afraid |
| travel |
| above |
| open |

© Pearson Education, Inc., 3

Home Activity Your child spelled words with the schwa sound (an unstressed vowel sound such as the *a* in *above*). Have your child pick a number between 1 and 15. Read the list word with that number and ask your child to spell it.

Name _____

Schwa

Spelling Words				
above	another	upon	animal	paper
open	family	travel	afraid	nickel
sugar	circus	item	gallon	melon

Proofread a Description Jake wrote about an imaginary animal. Circle four words that are spelled incorrectly and two words that should be combined into one compound word. Write the words correctly.

My anamal looks like a lizard with opun wings. It has beutiful colors. It lives above the tree tops. For food it breaks open a mellon. It is not afraid of any thing.

Frequently Misspelled Words

upon
again
beautiful

1. _____ 2. _____ 3. _____

4. _____ 5. _____ 6. _____

Proofread Words Fill in a circle to show which word is spelled correctly. Write the word.

7. There was an _____ in the paper about our class. 7. _____

 ○ itam ○ itum ○ item

8. Are you _____ you might get lost on the subway? 8. _____

 ○ afraid ○ ifraid ○ afriad

9. There are five people in my _____ . 9. _____

 ○ family ○ famaly ○ familie

10. The candy cost a _____ each. 10. _____

 ○ nicle ○ nickle ○ nickel

© Pearson Education, Inc., 3

 School + Home 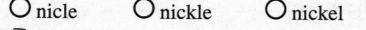 **Home Activity** Your child identified misspelled words with the schwa sound (an unstressed vowel sound such as the *a* in *above*). Give clues about a list word. Ask your child to guess and spell the word.

Name _____

Final Syllables

Opposites Write the missing list word. It will be the opposite of the underlined word.

1. The hero in this book lives in a <u>shack</u>.

1. _____

2. At first, I had trouble with <u>multiplication</u>.

2. _____

3. Let me interrupt with a <u>statement</u> about wind power.

3. _____

4. Jed left for his <u>usual job</u>.

4. _____

5. This story is <u>true</u>.

5. _____

Context Clues Write the last word of the sentence.

6. The situation called for quick _____.

7. The school nurse tested everyone's _____.

8. Her cheery smile is her best _____.

9. In art class, Tami made a plaster _____.

10. Please come to my birthday _____.

11. We bought some used _____.

12. An armadillo is an odd _____.

13. We walked in the wrong _____.

14. The toy robots had a _____.

15. Nature was important in the Aztec _____.

© Pearson Education, Inc., 3

Home Activity Your child wrote words that end with *-tion*, *-sion*, and *-ture*. Have your child underline these endings in the list words.

Name _____

Final Syllables

Spelling Words				
question	creature	furniture	division	collision
action	direction	culture	vacation	mansion
fiction	feature	sculpture	vision	celebration

Proofread a Description Gina's class is studying local history. Circle four spelling errors. Write the words correctly. Then write the two incomplete sentences as one sentence.

Mr. and Mrs. Hill we're very important in the history of our town. They built the Hill manshun in 1880. It still has the original furnichure. Many people tour the house when they are on vacasion. My favorite feature. Is the dolphin sculpture.

1. _____   2. _____

3. _____   4. _____

5. _____

Proofread Words Circle the word that is spelled correctly. Write it.

6. I have a   question   quesion.   6. _____

7. It's fun to learn about a new   calture   culture.   7. _____

8. An eagle has excellent   vishun   vision.   8. _____

9. We had a big   celebration   celebrasion.   9. _____

10. Which   direction   direcsion   is the library?   10. _____

Home Activity Your child identified misspelled words that end with *-tion*, *-sion*, and *-ture*. Give clues about a list word. Ask your child to guess and spell the word.

Name _____

Multisyllabic Words

Spelling Words				
leadership	gracefully	refreshment	uncomfortable	overdoing
remarkable	carefully	unbearably	ownership	unacceptable
impossibly	reappeared	unprepared	oncoming	misbehaving

Missing Syllables Add the missing syllables and write the list words.

1. The deer moved grace_____.   1. _____

2. He was ___bear___ rude.   2. _____

3. Watch out for ___com___ cars.   3. _____

4. That is a ___mark___ carving!   4. _____

5. Juice is my favorite ___fresh___.   5. _____

6. Sam is ___fort___ in crowds.   6. _____

7. Do the addition care_____.   7. _____

8. He took a lead_____ position.   8. _____

9. She gets tired from ___do___.   9. _____

10. Sue was ___pos___ stubborn.   10. _____

Definitions Write the list word with the same meaning as the underlined words.

11. He was <u>not prepared</u> for the test.   11. _____

12. The sun <u>appeared again</u> from behind the clouds.   12. _____

13. The puppy kept <u>behaving badly</u>.   13. _____

14. My score on the test was <u>not acceptable</u>.   14. _____

15. He claimed <u>to be the owner</u> of the stray cat.   15. _____

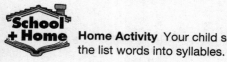

Home Activity Your child spelled words with many syllables. Have your child draw lines to divide the list words into syllables.

Multisyllabic Words

Spelling Words				
leadership	gracefully	refreshment	uncomfortable	overdoing
remarkable	carefully	unbearably	ownership	unacceptable
impossibly	reappeared	unprepared	oncoming	misbehaving

Proofread an Explanation Olivia wrote about how to bowl. Circle four spelling errors. Write the words correctly. Then add the missing comma.

Bowling is a remarkable sport. Almost every body likes it.

You should start with good equipment. Don't use a ball that is unbareably heavy and don't settle for unconfortable shoes.

When it's your turn, swing the ball back gracefully as you walk toward the pins. Let go when you reach the line. Always aim carefuly at the pins.

Frequently Misspelled Words
everybody everything

1. _____   2. _____

3. _____   4. _____

Correct the Words Write the correct spelling of each misspelled word.

5. unaceptable   5. _____

6. oncomeing   6. _____

7. missbehaving   7. _____

8. inpossibly   8. _____

9. reapeared   9. _____

10. leedership   10. _____

© Pearson Education, Inc., 3

School + Home **Home Activity** Your child is learning to spell words with many syllables. Have your child write a sentence using two or more of the list words.

Name _____

Related Words

Spelling Words				
cloth	clothes	nature	natural	able
ability	mean	meant	deal	dealt
please	pleasant	sign	signal	signature

Replacing Words Write list words to take the place of the underlined words.

1. I jumped out of the tub and put on my <u>shirt and shorts</u>.

   1. _____

2. It has been a <u>nice</u> day.

   2. _____

3. Did you <u>write your name on</u> the card?

   3. _____

4. Dogs have the <u>skill</u> to hear high-pitched sounds.

   4. _____

5. Mom made a kerchief from a scrap of blue <u>fabric</u>.

   5. _____

6. Tom is never <u>cruel</u> to animals.

   6. _____

7. We went to the mountains to enjoy <u>the environment</u>.

   7. _____

8. Sara <u>gave</u> six cards to each player.

   8. _____

Missing Words Write the missing word.

9. She has a _____ talent for music.

10. His hand _____ warned me to stop.

11. A bat is the only mammal that is _____ to fly.

12. That's not what I _____ .

13. I can do what I _____ on Saturday morning.

14. Her _____ is on the credit card.

15. My big sister knows how to _____ with most emergencies.

Home Activity Your child spelled related words. Have your child pronounce each list word and use the word in a sentence.

© Pearson Education, Inc., 3

112

Name _____

Related Words

Proofread a Paragraph Circle four spelling errors and cross out the sentence that does not belong in the paragraph. Write the words correctly.

> When I grow up, I whant to design clothes. I think I would be good at this. I have the abilty to draw, and I like to deal with people. I like to sketch outfits that pleese my friends. My best friend is Rosa. I am learning about cotton, wool, and other kinds of kloth.

Spelling Words

cloth
clothes
nature
natural
able
ability
mean
meant

deal
dealt
please
pleasant
sign
signal
signature

1. _____   2. _____

3. _____   4. _____

Frequently Misspelled Words

want
whole

Proofread Words Circle the word that is spelled correctly. Write it.

5. My bus driver is a **pleasant   plesant** person.

   _____

6. Wave to **signel   signal** if you need help.

   _____

7. Will you be **abel   able** to come to the party?

   _____

8. Simon was reading a book about the wonders of **nature   natur**.

   _____

School + Home **Home Activity** Your child spelled related words. Have your child point out a pair of related list words and explain how the spellings differ.

113

Vowel Sounds in *moon* and *foot*

Spelling Words				
few	school	true	goose	fruit
cookie	cushion	noodle	bookmark	balloon
suit	chew	glue	Tuesday	bushel

Word Clues Read the two meaning clues. Write the list word that the clues tell about.

1. a group of fish
   place where students learn

1. _____

2. a pillow
   to pad

2. _____

3. a sticky paste
   to paste something

3. _____

4. a toy filled with air
   to get bigger

4. _____

5. matched pieces of clothing
   to please or satisfy

5. _____

Meaning Connections Change the underlined word or words to a list word. Write the word.

6. I ate a chocolate chip <u>sweet treat</u>.

6. _____

7. A <u>bird that honks</u> chased me.

7. _____

8. Darla put a <u>paper placeholder</u> in the book.

8. _____

9. On <u>the day after Monday</u>, it rained.

9. _____

10. We bought <u>apples, grapes, and pears</u>.

10. _____

11. I saw a <u>piece of pasta</u> in my soup.

11. _____

12. I <u>chomp</u> on raw carrots for a snack.

12. _____

13. The farmer put corn in the <u>32-quart</u> basket.

13. _____

14. What she said was <u>not false</u>.

14. _____

15. <u>Not many</u> people can be called heroes.

15. _____

© Pearson Education, Inc., 3

 School + Home **Home Activity** Your child spelled words with the vowel sound in *moon* (spelled *oo, ew, ue, ui*) and in *foot* (spelled *oo, u*). Play Tic-Tac-Toe. One person chooses a word for the other person to spell. If the person spells the word correctly, he or she marks an X or an O on the grid.

Name _____

Schwa

Spelling Words				
above	another	upon	animal	paper
open	family	travel	afraid	nickel
sugar	circus	item	gallon	melon

Classifying Write the list word that belongs with each pair of words.

1. penny, dime, ___

2. pint, quart, ___

3. go, journey, ___

4. movie, play, ___

5. thing, object, ___

6. below, beside, ___

7. group, tribe, ___

1. _____

2. _____

3. _____

4. _____

5. _____

6. _____

7. _____

Complete the Phrase Write the list word that completes each phrase.

8. not a plant but an ___

9. a pencil and some ___

10. not a berry but a ___

11. not closed but ___

12. not under but ___

13. as sweet as ___

14. ___ of the dark

15. one thing and ___

Riddle Write the letters from the boxes above to find the answer to the riddle.

What do you get when you ask a lemon for help?

___ ___ ___ ___ ___ ___ ___ ___

Home Activity Your child learned to spell words with the schwa sound (an unstressed vowel sound such as the *a* in *about*). Take turns choosing and spelling a word. Then each of you say a word you associate with the chosen word: *family—Mom, Dad*.

Final Syllables

Spelling Words

question	creature	furniture	division	collision
action	direction	culture	vacation	mansion
fiction	feature	sculpture	vision	celebration

Crossword Puzzle Write the list word that each clue describes.

Across

1. north
5. a make-believe story
6. a statue
8. Aztec or Native American
9. a special trip
10. sight

Down

1. repeated subtraction
2. a big, big house
3. a party
4. a movement
5. chairs and sofas
7. an important part

Alphabetizing Read the two guide words. Write the list word that would come between them in a dictionary.

13. pride _____ rate
14. cave _____ comet
15. cracker _____ crop

collision
question
creature

© Pearson Education, Inc., 3

School + Home

Home Activity Your child spelled words that end with *-tion*, *-sion*, and *-ture*. Use newspapers or junk mail to look for words with the lesson endings. Circle the words and spell them together. Check to see if any circled words are on the spelling list.

Name _____

Multisyllabic Words

Spelling Words				
leadership	gracefully	refreshment	uncomfortable	overdoing
remarkable	carefully	unbearably	ownership	unacceptable
impossibly	reappeared	unprepared	oncoming	misbehaving

Word Building Read the word in dark type. Add the part or parts to the given word. Write the list word you make.

1. **grace** + suffix + suffix _____

2. prefix + **appear** + ending _____

3. **remark** + suffix _____

4. prefix + **comfort** + suffix _____

5. prefix + **accept** + suffix _____

6. **care** + suffix + suffix _____

7. prefix + **prepare** + ending _____

8. prefix + **fresh** + suffix _____

9. **lead** + suffix + suffix _____

10. **own** + suffix + suffix _____

Finish the Phrase Circle the list word that completes each phrase. Write it. Say the word. Write in the box the number of syllables you hear in the word.

11. (unprepared   unbearably) hot _____ ☐

12. (overdoing   reappeared) it a bit _____ ☐

13. (oncoming   unprepared) traffic _____ ☐

14. (leadership   misbehaving) puppy _____ ☐

15. (impossibly   carefully) difficult problem _____ ☐

Total ☐

Syllable Addition Add the numbers in the boxes. If you get 19, you did a great job!

Home Activity Your child is learning to spell words with many syllables. Together, say each word and clap the syllables. Let your child pick the three words he or she finds most difficult. Have your child write them and spell them to you.

Related Words

```
                  Spelling Words
   cloth     clothes    nature    natural   able
   ability   mean       meant     deal      dealt
   please    pleasant   sign      signal    signature
```

Word Pairs Write the list words that complete each sentence.

1.–2. Here is a STOP _____, and there is a traffic _____.

3.–4. My new _____ are made from colorful _____.

5.–6. Plants in _____ are _____ things.

7.–8. After you _____ the cards, they have been _____.

9.–10. If you _____ your name, you are using your _____.

Little Crosswords Read the word clue. Write a synonym for the word in the boxes going across. Write a related word in the boxes going down.

11.–12. skill

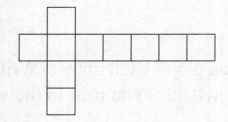

15.–16. nice

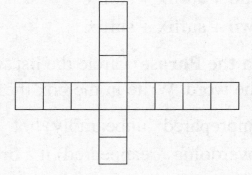

13.–14. intended

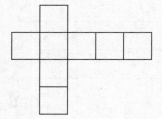

© Pearson Education, Inc., 3